SOFTWARE PROJECT ESTIMATION

INTELLIGENT FORECASTING, PROJECT CONTROL, AND CLIENT RELATIONSHIP MANAGEMENT

Dimitre Dimitrov

Apress®

Software Project Estimation: Intelligent Forecasting, Project Control, and Client Relationship Management

Dimitre Dimitrov
Toronto, ON, Canada

ISBN-13 (pbk): 978-1-4842-5024-2   ISBN-13 (electronic): 978-1-4842-5025-9
https://doi.org/10.1007/978-1-4842-5025-9

Managing Director, Apress Media LLC: Welmoed Spahr
Acquisitions Editor: Shiva Ramachandran
Development Editor: Rita Fernando
Coordinating Editor: Rita Fernando

Cover designed by eStudioCalamar

Author photo by Caroline Acton

Distributed to the book trade worldwide by Springer Science+Business Media New York, 233 Spring Street, 6th Floor, New York, NY 10013. Phone 1-800-SPRINGER, fax (201) 348-4505, e-mail orders-ny@springer-sbm.com, or visit www.springeronline.com. Apress Media, LLC is a California LLC and the sole member (owner) is Springer Science + Business Media Finance Inc (SSBM Finance Inc). SSBM Finance Inc is a **Delaware** corporation.

For information on translations, please e-mail rights@apress.com, or visit http://www.apress.com/rights-permissions.

Apress titles may be purchased in bulk for academic, corporate, or promotional use. eBook versions and licenses are also available for most titles. For more information, reference our Print and eBook Bulk Sales web page at http://www.apress.com/bulk-sales.

Any source code or other supplementary material referenced by the author in this book is available to readers on GitHub via the book's product page, located at www.apress.com/9781484250242. For more detailed information, please visit http://www.apress.com/source-code.

Printed on acid-free paper

To a friend.

"Invert, always invert"
—Carl Jacobi, 19th-century mathematician

Contents

About the Author

Dimitre Dimitrov is a software industry professional with 20 years of experience in project management, information systems development, and agile team coaching and facilitation. Dimitre has helped companies in a wide range of industries. He explores the forces and relationships that shape the lives of modern software development teams and their clients.

Acknowledgments

I am thankful to many of my colleagues for getting to this wonderful place of having written a book. I met some very bright programmers and managers who helped me see the right ways of approaching project planning and management—want to thank all the teams and clients I have worked with for being open to new ideas. I want to thank those who showed me the wrong ways as well.

And I want to thank my family, my lovely wife and girls, for having the chance to enjoy life together, and my sister and brother-in-law, for their deck, on which I wrote some of the pages of my book and felt as a true book author, basking in the summer sun and smelling the air of the Atlantic Ocean.

Special thanks to my editors and proofreaders. And special thanks to the owner of the Page One cafe in Toronto, whose place and atmosphere are inspiring many people to start their first page and where I claimed "I'm going to write a book."

Introduction

Why This Book?

Have you been on projects where halfway down the road it seems increasingly unlikely that you will finish as desired, but you can't put your finger on it and simply push through with a growing resentment? Have you been in meetings where scope discussions get increasingly difficult and depressing, ultimately sucking the energy out of everyone instead of enabling them to move forward with certainty and determination? Wouldn't it be good if a confident assertion for the project's ability to deliver is made as early as 1 or 2 months into the effort? What additional value and quality of working relationships can you generate if the time for estimation, tracking, and change management is slashed by a factor of 10 while simultaneously providing clients and team members with true peace of mind so they can focus on other important business activities? This book provides a practical tool that will help with all of this—it is a how-to book. But ultimately it is about the relationships we develop during projects and the appreciation of our colleagues and business partners.

It is 2019! Yet estimation and forecasting in the software development industry are still considered mystifying at best, and an archaic and obsolete concept at worst. Reliable forecasting continues to present a challenge for many teams and software development organizations. The practices associated with the two predominant software development methodologies are inadequate. Methods related to waterfall development are notoriously bad for long-term forecasting because they encourage too much information processing too early and have a tendency to skew reality into a Gantt chart. And methods that relate well to agile software development are not as notoriously bad, however, mostly because long-term forecasting is avoided altogether. This is problematic in many cases because it pushes important decisions too late in the project, adds unnecessary stress on people's relationships, and ultimately diminishes the chances for successful projects.

When forecasting is done on projects utilizing agile software development, it is often with short-term commitments—an iteration or a few at best. Such small-span commitments have minimal value for business people who want to look a year or two ahead. When teams practicing agile software development commit to a longer-term delivery, they suffer many of the same issues as people working on waterfall projects do—the desired "project targets" get missed, and there is lack of confidence throughout the project about what will be delivered and when. Senior businessmen and business-women lose the capacity to trust the delivery teams and organizations. People who work together for years remain at a distance and never build true partnerships. Many business teams and development teams are openly adversary.

One reason behind much of these issues is the inability for meaningful long-term commitment. And while reliably providing accurate and precise software estimates is close to impossible, reliably providing accurate and precise fore-casts is not. This book shows you how to do this and commit to a purpose early. A satisfactory solution can be reached with a small investment in under-standing people's problems and through the adoption of simple statistical principles. The security and reliability that you will be able to contribute to projects will improve your team's performance, morale, and motivation and will have a positive impact on long and healthy client relationships.

Who Is the Reader of This Book and What Can You Find in It?

Software Project Estimation is for anyone who wants to have a fresh and ade-quate outlook on the process of software estimation and forecasting, and how these activities facilitate the conversations and relationships among peo-ple. It is directly relevant to the roles of scrum masters and project managers and provides practical tools for intelligent project control. The book is also valuable for business people who want insight into the type of problems that delivery teams face, and for programmers and other delivery team members who want to gain an understanding of the project manager's day-to-day chal-lenges. While life experience as a member of a software project is useful for quickly recognizing some of the situational nuances, this book will appeal to curious people who are early in their careers.

The described forecasting method relies on the ability of a technical team to deliver working software with consistency. Many of the technical practices enabling such delivery have been perfected and popularized by what came to be known as agile software development. Thus, in practice, the forecasting and control methods align well with the operational mode of many teams delivering software with an agile development methodology. However, this is not a book about agile software development. If you and your team are prac-ticing solid software development and do not label yourself as agile or extreme, then this book will be valuable for you too.

Estimation by itself is of limited use. We do it to forecast and plan. Forecasting and planning are in turn done to improve the chances of making good deci-sions and taking appropriate actions. A forecast does not improve a project's performance. It is only a tool for visualizing that performance. This book shows how to use an intelligent forecast for making timely decisions and applying measured project control for steering toward a valuable goal.

Before going any deeper in this book, we need to establish that estimation and forecasting are two different things. This book is more about forecasting and control. However, the term "estimation" has been misused for so long that it has become the normal term for describing what amounts to forecasting. Estimation is only the initial guess about the size of something. Forecasting is the activity of processing input data, including the estimates, and formulating an intelligent prediction.

Where this book ventures into a longer treatment on a subject, or establishes an explicit view on the meaning of a concept, it is not done with the intent to educate the reader, rather it is done with the intent of providing context so the reader can align their understanding with the ideas in the book. For more information on some of the relevant concepts, you can refer to the literature provided in the Bibliography at the end.

The method presented here scales well over software projects with different sizes, provided the organizational structure and the development methods are such that continuously delivering working software is achieved.

Small projects consisting of a few developers working for a couple of months are harder to control through the approach provided by this book, but you can still find useful ideas to guide your future discussions with clients and teammates.

In the context of a legacy system, the applicability of the approach depends on whether the system is healthy or not, or at least on how homogeneously unpredictable is working on the system. For projects within healthy legacy systems, you can apply the concepts almost directly. For projects within legacy systems with compromised codebase integrity, you can cherry-pick ideas that make sense in your context and apply them when there is an opportunity.

This book will be of particular value to people who provide software project delivery as a service to other companies or departments within larger organizations. Teams utilizing modern development techniques and automation have often achieved the technical excellence required for reliable forecasting and intelligent project control. These teams often serve big corporate clients who are not well dispositioned or are downright allergic to the concept of no estimation and no long-term planning. By providing a viable alternative to the Gantt chart as a control method, this book will help delivery teams speak the language of business people without sacrificing software development performance or quality of delivery practices.

Finally, *Software Project Estimation* will provide clues for achieving a mind-set that allows us to bridge an important gap—to see each other (delivery teams and clients) as human and to appreciate each other's and our own needs, abilities, and expectations.

#NoEstimates

Since this book has the word "estimation" in its title, it seems appropriate to address the idea of #NoEstimates.

#NoEstimates is about searching for alternatives to estimates. The method described in this book might actually fall in this category of alternative to the broadly accepted methods of estimation. However, it can be also seen as a logical extension of traditional estimation. I will leave it to the reader to make their own judgment as to whether the method described here is alternative or not—if that categorization matters to the reader at all.

Exploring alternatives is interesting when context is maintained. Still, much of the discussions in the #NoEstimates blogs and articles move haphazardly from project delivery to product development to software development. These are vastly different contexts. The book you are reading is about estimating, forecasting, and controlling software projects.

In contrast, the concepts of business value and guided product experiments are primarily about product development. Software quality, continual integration, and automation are primarily about software engineering. All three—product delivery, software delivery, and project delivery—are complementary, and when done right each draws on the strengths of the others. While product delivery and software delivery present just as interesting and important problems, they are not the main subject of this book and are only examined where it facilitates the discussion of intelligent project forecasting.

How Is This Book Organized?

The concepts in the book build upon each other. Concepts covered earlier are needed to fully appreciate those covered later. Ideally the reader will take on a sequential approach and read the book from front to back.

That said, many of the sections in the book can be read without having read the previous sections or chapters. Some readers might be familiar with a few of the ideas presented in this book and could dive straight into a later chapter. The sections within chapters are kept brief, making it easier to locate topics when reading nonsequentially.

Chapter 0 initializes a minimalistic context for the rest of the book.

Chapters 1–3 lay out the topography.

Chapter 4 describes the core estimation and forecasting techniques.

Chapters 5 and 6 add important details.

Appendix A is a compilation of ideas and techniques that are important for supporting the practical application of this method.

Appendix B contains a few spreadsheet examples.

Frequently Used Pronouns, Collective Nouns, and Terms

A few words appear repeatedly throughout the text:

"People" is often used as all the people on a project, which includes both client and the software delivery team. Or, "people" can sometimes refer to only one of these groups—either the client team or the software delivery team.

"We" is mainly from the perspective of the software delivery team, but it is also used from the perspective of all the people involved on a software project. Occasionally "we" stands for project managers and scrum masters only.

"Business people" and "client" are used for the people who request the software solution. Sometimes these people are external clients, and sometimes they are from another department within the same company.

"Software developers" is generally meant as the programmers, designers, and testers from the delivery team, but is sometimes used to describe all the people who contribute to the delivery of a software project, including the scrum master and project manager.

"The team" and "project team"—these and similar expressions are used to mean all the people on a project, including people from the client team who are actively engaged with the project.

"Delivery team" is basically "the project team" less the "business people."

If there are five scrum teams working on the same project, then all of these are considered "the delivery team," since the major discussion in this book focuses on estimating and forecasting complete projects and not individual team's performance.

"Accurate" is generally used to mean both accurate and precise, since we are only interested in the pragmatic side of forecasting.

"Project" is a collaborative enterprise for achieving a particular valuable goal over a set period (and within certain limitations).

"Project management" is meant as the activities related to decision making and application of control over project parameters in a way that is most conducive to the project's success. It also includes the activities related to securing the people's well-being within the project boundaries.

"Project manager" is generally meant to describe a role and not a job title. Anyone who is participating in project management activities on the project can play the project manager's role. A scrum master can often be a project manager, but so can a team lead, a director, or a manager. Occasionally, the whole team can be the project manager.

"Project performance" captures the project's progress toward success in terms of delivered functionality and expanded effort. It is not exactly the same as team performance, although both are certainly related. It is important to keep in mind that the definition of success might shift during a typical project as people adjust to reality.

Assertions

These are the beliefs and assertions which give meaning to much of the discussion in this book.

"Certainty or safety is a basic need"—At some level every person needs safety. At the most elementary level, a person needs physical and psychological safety. This is true even when a person engages in an inherently risky endeavor like starting a new software project.

"A software team can deliver continuously within a controlled productivity range"—Modern delivery teams have mastered proven software engineering practices and have repeatedly demonstrated that their productivity can remain within constant limits throughout the duration of a project. We will take "constant limits" to mean that if there are two comparable pieces of functionality, then the team will complete these by expanding comparable amounts of effort, and we can expect this to hold true throughout the project (with the possible exception of the first few weeks when people are picking up speed).

"Project control is more important than record keeping"—On a software project, the primary responsibility of anyone involved is to take actions with the intent to control and steer the project to success. Bookkeeping is of secondary or ternary importance. The benefit of forecasting is to pull certain important decisions earlier in the project's life. We are not forecasting to prove something right or wrong, nor are we estimating to keep a record and hold people accountable for the estimation numbers they produced.

© Dimitre Dimitrov 2020
D. Dimitrov, *Software Project Estimation*,
https://doi.org/10.1007/978-1-4842-5025-9_1

"It is only worth forecasting when there is ability to act"—A forecast on its own does not change the outcome of a project. There must be a real possibility that we make control decisions, which lead to measured and timely actions, and change the project's parameters. If such readiness for action does not exist on a project, and will never exist regardless of new knowledge, then forecasting becomes useless.

The People in a Software Project

Let's start this book with a short stroll around the office to meet the people who are involved in a software project. It is important to look at their typical problems and desires so that we have confidence in the adequacy of the forecasting method and the approach to project control that we develop later in this book. It is the people, with their problems and desires, who establish the solution's adequacy.

The People

The client (a.k.a. business person). These are the people who generate business solutions. They take business risks, sometimes having to power through considerable fears and doubt. They hustle and discover valuable things that other people need and are willing to pay for. Their ideas and resolve for action accomplish the visionary work needed for the creation of something new. Sometimes they need software tools in order to move their business ideas forward. Even when they take on a project for building a software solution, they are not software developers, rather they are business developers.

© Dimitre Dimitrov 2020
D. Dimitrov, *Software Project Estimation*,
https://doi.org/10.1007/978-1-4842-5025-9_2

The developer (a.k.a. programmer, tester, designer). These are the people whose brains and hands perform the implementation work and bring a software solution into existence. They are skilled in software techniques and in making computer systems perform complex things. They understand how users interact with software. Many of these people can keep large amounts of information and abstractions in their brains. They enjoy seeing these abstractions materialize in the form of working software and sharing this miracle with the rest of us. A certain element of playfulness and doing things purely for the sake of having them done can be found in many software developers.

The project manager and the scrum master. These are the people charged with facilitating and organizing various project activities. They help other people make decisions and thus have an effect on how a project is being controlled. Key activities affecting decision making on a project are forecasting and scope control. While project managers and scrum masters do not themselves produce estimates, they play a central role[1] in how these estimates are used into planning, and subsequently how the plans are enacted throughout the project's execution. The facilitation work that project managers and scrum masters perform is critical for the overall project tone and the quality of the work environment.

The product owner and the business analyst. These are the people who have the skill of converting the ideas of business people into a format consumable by software developers. Product owners can also make confident decisions on what is valuable and what is less valuable in a software solution. Business analysts, and many product owners, help describe, and to a degree define, the solution that brings about the capabilities desired by business people. Their work greatly affects the quality of information that developers get to process, the volume of implementation work, and the end product suitability.

The manager and the team lead. These are the people who are tasked with getting the job done. They manage teams of developers with finite capabilities and less finite potential and are responsible for creating the environment where developers can do their work well. These are also often the people who provide initial estimates for software projects. They may delegate the actual estimation to their teams, but they remain personally

---

[1] Technically, scrum masters are absolved from the responsibility of planning out the full project. They only focus on helping the team work better and remove impediments. However, I consider client discomfort and uncertainty to be major impediments for the team's work. As such, the scrum master is responsible for minimizing them. One of the things that can be done is to have a better project forecast, reliable long-term commitment, and a working plan for effective project control.

accountable for the information that gets communicated to clients. When it comes to project sizing, Managers and Team Leads are often expected to use experience and gut intuition for producing an overall project estimate that is safe and sufficiently accurate.

The Problems

A problem is something to be worked out or solved, but it is also something that allows people to self-validate and to ultimately grow as human beings. The way a person approaches their own problems has a noticeable effect on their quality of life and those around them. The way one person approaches other people's problems has a noticeable effect on the trust and relationships they will be able to establish.

Making a decision. This is one of the main problems for businessmen and businesswomen. Making decisions is how they make their living and create the ecosystems for other people to make their livelihood too. The actual mechanics of deciding is not what creates difficulty for them, but it is the build-up to that decision which costs them time, effort, and comfort. It is a complex problem since the business context involves various bits of information and many unknowns that are all in flux. Business people deal with this complexity and handle the unknown by taking risks and venturing into business experiments.

The challenge that software projects present is the high variability of just about everything—which basically translates into more uncertainty. Some feel uncertainty is what business is all about.

Making a promise. This is one of the main problems for makers. Software developers are makers. People who make things with their minds and hands love seeing the products of their labor being used by others. Makers enjoy providing solutions to other people's problems. A maker wants to say "I will solve your problem. Just tell me what it is."

Whether the promise is explicit or implicit, it is real, and both the maker and the client appreciate its power. How to make the promise carry through is the problem that makers wrestle with.

Making a plan. Making a plan is a problem for anyone who is accountable for seeing a project to an end. On software development projects, this is often the person tasked with project management responsibilities.

One way or another, every project ends. What activities happen between the start of a project and the end of a project, and what is the result of each of these activities, ultimately have a crucial impact on whether the project ends successfully or not. Consequently, identifying the activities with the best chance of contributing to a successful outcome is of primary interest for a planner.

Typically, there is an expectation, or at least a wish, for a reliable plan to be in place sooner rather than later through the life of a project. Even when the "plan" is to simply work through the mountain of challenges, the project manager is expected to guide the effort on a path of success and to have sufficient foresight into why the chosen path is the one leading to success.

WHO CARES!

It is easy to say "Don't promise" and "Don't plan." It is less easy to say "Don't make decisions," although some people do say it in a roundabout way. Even though these approaches look seductively simple, and there is a hint of bravery in choosing them, none leads to a satisfactory solution. They invariably lead to unwelcome compromises that people need to accept at the expense of comfort and happiness.

In the context of a single project, managers have a similar problem to planners; they want to see the project on time. And business analysts have a similar problem to makers, that is, they need to see their work materialize and produce valuable results.

The Desires

An adequate solution should solve a problem and align with desires. So let's make a few more generalizations. You will notice this as a pattern that applies to estimation and forecasting too—by making careful simplifications we can get good enough understanding of a complex problem.

To make decisions on reliable information. For business people this is one of the primary desires. By the nature of what they do, they need to make so many decisions that any opportunity for making a quick and clear decision, based on little but reliable information, is welcome.

The next best thing is the knowledge that reliable information will be available at a defined moment in time. When businessmen and businesswomen are faced with uncertainty, they can tolerate it for a while, but it helps them a lot if they have an idea of what to expect once the waiting is over.

Why is this important? It is important so that we can properly sequence the input we are providing to people who are making decisions. We need to appreciate what suits them best at a given moment in the life of the project.

This makes communications much more meaningful and allows us to move through seemingly difficult situations with ease.

To be able to work. Makers and artists, which software engineers are, enjoy working. They like being useful and spending time tinkering with whatever happens to be in their field of interest. What they typically don't enjoy is to deal with something they cannot perceive to be real, valuable, and true. They markedly dislike the situations where they are the originator of things with questionable worth.

For makers, it is preferable to describe a complex problem in a complex way, rather than sacrifice the truth and provide simplistic and untrue answer. Makers can bend a little and deal with uncertainty, but only for short periods of time. They prefer to spend their time making things.

Why is this important? Because it is important to understand that software developers detest estimation, and forecasting by extension, since they cannot be proven to be true. They are only a guess. And for makers a guess represents little value. For this reason, we need to be sensitive and empathetic to their dislike when we need their input and cooperation. When developers see that we understand the binary unsustainability of our own request, they will oddly be more willing to help. But it is also important for another reason—when developers see that our forecasting efforts are ultimately designed to provide them with a more sensible environment for work, there is a material improvement in the relationship's dynamics.

To be able to apply control. For people who make plans and who are responsible for delivering a project, like project managers, team leads, and scrum masters, it is highly desirable to have control over how things roll out toward the project objective. Of course, a project manager is not judged by their ability to strictly follow a rigid plan. Rather, the project manager is ultimately valued for their ability to deliver a satisfactory project, changing plans if necessary, and even steering in the absence of a ratified plan.

Guiding things along a known plan of action is typically easier than making all the right calls in real time without the benefit of planning and anticipation. A plan provides a useful reference and an opportunity to rehearse some scenarios in advance. It puts us in anticipatory mode and not in reactive mode of being. In this way we can roughly gauge if things are panning out well, and we can set interim course direction which helps us move through obstacles without getting distracted by too much fear and unnecessary considerations. The more control a planner can exert on how work is being completed during the execution of a project, the more likely it is the end result agrees with the plan and, by assumption (please see the side note), with the expectations and wants of the people affected by the project.

PROJECT MANAGEMENT? SO 20TH CENTURY!

Waterfall is a method for software development and project management, which relies heavily on thorough and exhaustive preplanning. It has come to be that Waterfall is a bad thing in many cases, mainly for not being able to adjust to reality. Planning and software project management, as practices, have been associated with Waterfall for so long that many people treat them as equivalent. We need to separate them though, because they are not the same. There are ways to plan and to manage a project that are dramatically different than what Waterfall has established as a standard.

The Manifesto for Agile Software Development (`https://agilemanifesto.org/`)[2] says we (the software developers) value responding to change over following a plan. Suggesting that following the plan might be the better thing to do sounds like a contradiction to the manifesto. However, there are two assumptions, or rather oversimplifications, which are baked into this particular postulate of the Manifesto for Agile Software Development. The first is that we value responding to change only when we have assessed that the change merits a response. We are not merely responding to any change that comes along. The other is that we value responding to change over following a *static* plan, not over following a plan in general. A plan can be revisited and adjusted (even within the constraints of a contract). When the plans adapt to the relevant changes in reality, we can confidently follow these plans, while simultaneously responding to change.

Here, we are talking about effective project control—steering the project reliably into producing the desired outcomes. For example, having power control over people's overtime is not effective control in this sense, while minimizing context switching by suggesting or enforcing a smaller WIP (work in progress) rule, or by improving feedback time, can be considered an application of adequate project control.

---

[2] See Appendix A for a more detailed discussion about the manifesto.

WHAT CONTROL?

In this book, when we talk about control, we are talking about *project control.* And we are explicitly not talking about control over people.

There are three primary project controls we can manipulate:

- **Scope**—controls the "what" of the solution

- **Effort**—represents the power we apply toward building the solution

- **Duration**—represents the time we have available for finishing the project

By adjusting each of these controls within the project envelope, we can affect the project's progress and ultimately can drive the project toward desired objectives. There are other project aspects that can be recognized as distinct secondary controls. They have direct and indirect impact on the primary controls, and they are also very important in their own right for managing the less tangible outcomes of a project. These are the Environment, Software Quality, Metrics, and Value.

Environment, the well-being and collaborative capacity of people, can be treated as a secondary control. It almost directly converts to Effort— motivated people deliver more effectively. In this sense Environment can be considered part of the Effort primary control, and by improving the environment, we increase the available effort that can be expanded toward the project goal.

Software Quality, the well-being and capacity for change in the code base, can also be treated as a secondary control. However, for most teams this is only a theoretical control since the quality that the team can attain is constant (and maximum) within the envelope of a single project. Lowering the quality is of course possible, but it cannot be considered a control since it doesn't make sense. In any case, improving software quality, if it can be done sustainably within the project, also translates to Effort because once the team is working at an improved quality level, they get to expend less effort for achieving a comparable result.

Metrics, the health of the adopted development processes. Driving toward more controlled processes improves the predictability of events on the project and the likelihood of a forecast being close to the actual outcome. To the extent that an improved process can be proven to facilitate better productivity, we can consider it an effective project control. However, let's not forget that individuals and interactions come before processes and tools. Enforcing rigid processes will backfire when creativity and thinking are the primary activities of people (which is the case on software development projects).

Value of the end product. Prioritizing functionality, so that we first complete the more valuable pieces, is a critically important derisking technique. Prioritization is a variation of the scope control. Occasionally people will discover valuable functionality that has not been previously recognized as an objective for the project. Pivoting for value represents *product control*, not project control. However, the value of the end result is so crucial for the project success that the project must accommodate changes to scope where this has been deemed the correct course of action. If the change in scope cannot be contained within the current project envelope, then the whole project needs to be reframed.

It should be noted that within the context of a given project, the appropriate and sufficient value is assumed to be guaranteed by the project's definition itself. A project starts with a specific goal, and it is expected that this goal has enough value to justify the project.

With forecasting we are seeking insight on where and when to apply *project control*.

Summary

There are a few typical roles on any software project. Sometimes these roles might be fulfilled by people whose daily roles are different. For example, a developer might be a maker primarily, but can double as a project manager and planner. It is less likely to see a business person play the role of a maker and deliver solid software code, but it is not unheard of.

Clients, developers, and facilitators (scrum masters, project managers, team leads) have various problems and desires. Most of the time they prefer to do what they do best. People don't mind occasionally spending time on things they do not consider their primary interest, and they don't mind temporarily hanging in suspense, but they seek the things that make them comfortable and happy. They desire some form of certainty and autonomy.

Outside these generalizations lies a diverse set of highly nuanced human wants, fears, and relationships. But the bulky characterizations we discussed in this chapter define the landscape on most software development projects.

The Role of Simplification

In this chapter we look at simplicity and explore why it is good to keep things simple. We will go over a few concepts that will allow us to view complex matter through simplified but correct models.

A model is a composition of ideas that help us understand a subject that the model represents. A correct model is one which introduces little or no skew to the particular aspect of interest, that is, there is a reliable mapping between what we understand through the model and what we would see if we were to look directly at the subject we are examining. A model can provide significant simplification and still be correct for a given purpose. For example, if we are considering shipping books through the mail, then modeling a book as a solid box with some weight might be a decent simplification.

An oversimplified model distorts reality in a way that makes the model unacceptable for what we are trying to accomplish. An overly complicated model is too hard to work with and is not worth the knowledge it provides—even if it's a correct model.

For example, if we model the book as simply a "unit," it might be oversimplified. Consider: "I will ship 4 units."—it doesn't carry the necessary information for size and weight. On the other hand: "I will ship 4 reading doohickeys, each consisting of two 6"x9" flat unbendable cardboard surfaces hinge-attached longitudinally along the 9 inch edges and encompassing a set of 250 collated

D. Dimitrov, *Software Project Estimation*,
https://doi.org/10.1007/978-1-4842-5025-9_3

flexible paper sheets suitable for printing" is overly complicated, useless, and probably wrong, even if we could derive the weight and size of each doohickey.

When looking for simple solutions, it is important to keep in mind that we still want a true representation of the reality. Sometimes, to stay true, we need to combine a few simple concepts and even build a more complex model—as long as it is not significantly more complex than it needs to be, the solution can be considered simple in the context of the specific problem.

Why is simplicity important in the context of software estimation, forecasting, and planning? One of the reasons is that these activities do not represent a primary interest for any of the people on the project. Business people want to make decisions and move on. Developers want to be working and creating software solutions. And project managers want the project to be rolling, and they want to be able to control it toward a successful outcome.

And while everyone on the project understands the importance of a schedule, it is not the schedule or the plan itself that makes anyone happy. Thus, it is best if this aspect of the project planning[1] is approached in a simple and painless way.

It is useful to examine simplicity on its own before we try to capture it within the specific techniques for estimation, forecasting, and planning. This will allow us to confidently accept the validity of the method discussed later. Whence this chapter.

What's Wrong with (Overly) Simple Answers?

Simple answers are very much okay and desirable when they reflect a similarly simple reality.

But software projects are rarely simple. Thus, providing a simple answer to almost any question about a software project risks oversimplification.

For example, let's consider the simple question, "When is this project going to end?" This can be easily answered by producing a calendar date—July 2nd. A simple answer like this leaves too many unanswered questions which are implied in the original inquiry. Is the project going to be successful? Is everyone going to feel it was a successful project or only some people? Is the

---

[1] It is important to distinguish between the portion of planning, which takes care of the schedule, and project planning in general. Project planning encompasses a diverse set of business activities which can be immensely interesting to many people. We are not talking about that planning here, and we will limit ourselves to discussing the part of it which deals with estimation, forecasting, and scheduling.

project goal going to be met fully or partially? Is there anything else that needs to happen for the project to be useful?

It is unlikely that someone on a project cares only about the end date. The reality for which people care is complex, and it is also constantly changing. Producing overly simple answers in this context is not adequate. But sometimes people get lazy and want to get rid of the problem with a silver bullet[2]—a single metric, or a single best practice, a single simple answer. And instead of simplifying the matter, they only introduce uncertainty, increase the likelihood of misunderstanding, and ultimately reduce the chances for a successful outcome.

What's Wrong with Complicated Answers?

Complicated answers do not instill trust. They require too much intellectual investment to be understood, and they are only adequate when everyone is deeply interested in the subject matter in question.

When producing a project forecast, we need to be careful with exposing the underlying complexities. People will increasingly doubt the forecasting method with each layer of complexity.

What people need is a simple and fast process—producing simple and trustworthy answers.

Complicated answers are not always unwanted. Some of the speculations we make during forecasting depend on nontrivial relationships among things. We want to hide these when possible, but if someone is explicitly inquiring about the source of our reasoning, we should be able to dive in and provide satisfactory answers regardless of how complicated the reality around them happens to be. In a scenario like this, maintaining simplicity will frustrate people more than inadvertently overcomplicating an answer.

Simple Constructs That Capture Complex Reality

Range. Range is the more adequate alternative of a singular value in almost any project context. For example, if a client asks "How long do you think this project will be?", an answer of "11 months" can be suspicious, while the equally simple answer of "Between 10 and 12 months" can be satisfactory and more adequate.

---

[2] Fred Brooks, "No Silver Bullet — Essence and Accidents of Software Engineering," *Proceedings of the IFIP Tenth World Computing Conference*, H.-J. Kugler, ed., Elsevier Science B.V. Amsterdam, NL (1986): 1069-76.

Ranges allow us to say things that are sufficiently true. These statements generate all the trust needed without exposing the underlying complexities and uncertainties.

Of course, if we answer "Between 6 and 16 months," we are just as correct (or more), but the uncertainty increases unacceptably. The client will have the same doubts as if we hadn't provided an answer at all, only now they will also question our ability to adequately understand their problems. The answer "Between 10 months and 20 days and 11 months and 10 days," which can be correct and very precise, triggers similar suspicions.

To build a meaningful range, we need to know the answers to two questions:

- What is an adequate accuracy for the listener? This can also be called "acceptable error." It is a value that represents how far off the true answer someone is willing to go and still consider the result good.

- What is a meaningful and sufficiently true value that the range should encompass?

Often, guessing is acceptable replacement for knowledge, so we don't really need to know the exact answers to the two questions, but only to be able to guess them with some level of comfort. Try this next time you are challenged to produce a seemingly simple answer, especially when it is about estimates and dates—instead of a number, produce a range. If people still insist on a singular answer, then use "most likely" and pick a value within the range. We talk about probabilities later.

Conditionals. Conditionals help us when there are a few possibilities that would make for an unacceptably wide range if we were to wrap them all into a single range.

Sometimes an answer can be dramatically different based on various factors. Instead of producing a single range encompassing the many possible outcomes, it is better to have an answer that represents the disparate possibilities.

For example, when talking to a client, instead of saying, "This project might take between 8 and 12 months," we can say, "This project will take between 10 and 12 months if we add Chris to the team. And it will take between 8 and 10 months if we add Avery."

By using conditionals we provide the client with a clearer picture at the expense of minimal extra complexity. The end result is a simple reality for the client.

If we spare the conditionals and provide a wider range, say "between 8 and 12 months" from the preceding example, we overload the listener with a different type of complexity—they need to consider whether the range is acceptable to them in its entirety. It may be that the project must end in less than 10 months. The client can wrongly assume that it is more likely for us to be on the upper end of the provided range, which is 12 months, and they can decide not to do the project with us. We were technically correct but didn't provide the needed information.

Boundary. Setting boundaries is an important technique for simplifying the reality and for staying safe. It is the emanation of responsibility. When we stay within reasonable boundaries, the people we work with get the healthy message that we are taking measures for our own safety, and as a result they tend to see us as more trustworthy. However, let's quickly consider what a reasonable boundary is and how does the nature of the work change the meaning of reasonable.

People often say "Don't drive beyond your headlights." This is as valid in software project context as anywhere else. When driving a car, it simply means to drive with a speed which allows you to stop on time when something enters the illuminated area ahead of you. When controlling a project, it simply means to only commit to what you have real information about.

One of the difficult things when communicating ideas is to make sure that other people understand accurately what we have in mind. For example, when we say that the estimates show it will take around 10 months to complete the project, it is likely that people understand this as "The project will take 10 months to complete." But what we said is that an estimate we made is 10 months, not the (actual) length of the project.

Let's see how setting a boundary can expose the important limits in our statements and help with this problem. We may say this instead: "We only have looked at the first two modules with enough detail to speculate on effort cost and duration. Based on what we have estimated, and on all the assumptions we made, we think it will take us 1.5 months to complete these two modules. We have identified a few risks as well. If you want us to discuss the assumptions or the identified risks, it can help us all stay more aligned through the next 2 months. If the projection for these two modules turns out correct, we will be comfortable forecasting the whole project at 16 to 18 months."

The boundaries we set in this statement are

- Only part of the system has been assessed.
- There are assumptions, so we only feel safe within them being true.

- The overall estimate is based on the smaller estimate being true.

- There are also some risks.

Now, it's true that the statement is not Twitter friendly.[3] But it sets boundaries within a relatively concise articulation, and these boundaries make it more likely that the client's understanding of what we said is closer to what we meant. A listener might need some extra time for processing it, and we might need to furnish help, but this extra time is in the order of minutes. If we spare the few minutes here and try to be short, we risk people working with incorrect understanding for months.

This is important because when we allow the discrepancies in people's understandings to accumulate for long periods, it drains their trust and will eventually exhaust it—people become convinced that there is no chance for common understanding. When this happens toward the end of a long and complex project, there might not be enough willpower left for discussing issues rationally and making collaborative decisions that work for everyone. Instead, it is likely that people start blaming each other. Someone will invariably say "But you said 12 months! We are now only 2 weeks from that!"—estimation and forecasting have turned into tools for assigning blame and controlling people, not tools for controlling projects.

Let's now see how the meaning of reasonable boundary can change based on the essence of the work. Consider the driving through the night analogy again. While we are driving the vehicle, it is reasonable to only stay within the headlights. It might be even more reasonable to stay within half of what the headlights cover. But let's imagine that we stop driving and take a short break on the side of the road. There is nothing wrong with envisioning how long it will take us to the next little town, so we can find a restaurant to eat, or how long it will take to cross a continent, if that's what the trip is about.

When the nature of our work is to envision the future, it becomes unproductive to maintain the same boundaries that make sense when we work on the immediate tasks propelling us toward that same vision.

When the future is unknown, we can still maintain enough limiting conditions—for example, we can say, "Provided we maintain the same pace, we will deliver the first phase of the project in 6 months, so 9 months in total. Based on the high-level specifications, it seems the second phase is similar in size,

---

[3] Many people these days take pride in emulating Steve Jobs and emit ridiculously succinct messages (in emails or otherwise), only to then have other people perform inordinate amount of juggling and mental trickery before finally arriving at the "correct" rendition of the intent in the commanding message. We need to be careful when pretending to be Steve Jobs!

and it is likely to take a similar amount of time, but this is a speculation which I'm not comfortable with at the moment."

We can share our fears and not push through by force and commitment only. Stated fear is a type of boundary, and we communicate that we are not willing to venture too far beyond it. This way we stake a claim into the unknown and still maintain boundaries that make sense to us. Opening up with our fears takes courage. And we show others that we are both brave and smart. It is important that we are brave at work, and it is also important to stay responsible. As we get more data, we can sharpen the boundaries and engage with commitments without fear.

Void. Void is the construct signifying the absence of something. The importance of this construct is that it allows us to not have to invent information about something that is simply not there.

When we can intelligently deal with uncomfortable situations, we are creating trust. It is much more responsible to acknowledge an (ideally temporary) inability to provide information than to supply fake data masquerading as information. Whether we work for other people or we risk our own money, being responsible is the behavior which creates and builds trust the most. Being irresponsible can destroy trust quicker than any other misstep, even when it doesn't cause material loss.

Business people can handle void fairly well if they know when information will be available. They can also handle cost associated with obtaining information sooner. The cost might be in money or in increased risk. This allows us to say: "I cannot provide meaningful information for the target date at the moment, but if we start now, with the team we considered, I can provide an outlook with 90% certainty in 2 months, and with 70% certainty in 4 weeks."

Business people are capable of managing this type of situation well, and provided we can supply the additional information as promised, void is more meaningful than something that we only wish to be true.

Probability. This leads us to the next construct—probability. Because it is such a central notion in estimation and forecasting, it has its own section in the next chapter. But let's quickly sketch it here as a tool for simplifying the reality and talk more about its other properties later.

Probability is in a way similar to a range. With a range we guarantee the value is within the upper and lower limits. With a probability we avoid providing that guarantee, but provide a measure of how likely it is that the actual value matches some target instead.

When it comes to software estimations, probabilities do translate to a range almost directly. For example, if I say, "I'm 80% certain the project will end 10 months from now," this can be translated like "The project will end between 10 and 12 months from now." Where if I say, "I'm 90% certain the project will end 10 months from now," then this can be interpreted as "The project will end between 10 and 11 months from now."

It is interesting to note that when we make software projections, we talk about things taking longer than expected and not shorter—"I'm 80% certain that the project will end 10 months from now" rarely means the project might turn out to be 8 months. There is an implied "at least" in front of the number of months—"I'm 80% certain that the project will end *at least* 10 months from now."

Summary

Software projects are complicated. However, there are communication tools we can use to simplify things considerably and still have a correct understanding of the relevant issues. These tools are common structures that make it easier for us to comprehend problems, to find and share options, and make decisions.

People have different demands for information and different tolerance levels to simplification. We need to learn how to use these simplification tools in ways that fit organically with everyone on the project—clients, developers, and managers. If we can help others feel more comfortable, then we can secure a better environment for effective collaboration.

Things need to stay as simple as possible, especially when it comes to estimation and forecasting. But sometimes we need to think beyond simplicity in order to capture it truly. We are discussing a few slightly more complex phenomena in the next chapter, and this gets us ready to start on the core of this book.

Statistics and Probabilities

In this chapter we touch on statistics and probabilities. We will look at a few interesting applications of statistics and will focus on how they affect decision making, because the main purpose of intelligent forecasting is to facilitate decision making and project control.

Probability

What is probability? What does it mean to you? For example, what does it mean if I say that you have 80% chance of making $100 profit when you invest $100?

It doesn't mean much as a number on its own. It doesn't tell us whether you will win $100 or not. It only starts meaning something when we put it in context of other things. For example, are you willing to take on the 20% probability that you lose $100? Do you only have $100 available? Are you only allowed to bet one time, two times, or more? Is it your goal to win the extra $100 in the first place? The answers to these questions provide real meaning to the probability number.

Probability is a number that helps us decide if we want to try something with the intent of obtaining a certain outcome. If we are not interested in the specific outcome, the probability number is of only superficial interest. But if we do care about the outcome, then this number starts having a more material meaning.

© Dimitre Dimitrov 2020

D. Dimitrov, *Software Project Estimation*,

https://doi.org/10.1007/978-1-4842-5025-9_4

When we talk about a singular event, probability represents a binary reality—something either happens or it doesn't happen. The probability number informs us how likely are we to win or lose. If we are willing to take the risk of losing, we might proceed. If the risk is too high, or the potential prize too insignificant, we might choose to not proceed. But regardless of the likelihood, if we decide to proceed, we still either win or lose. See Figure 3-1.

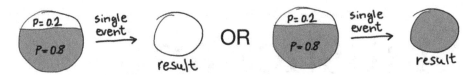

Figure 3-1. P=0.2 means there is 20% probability for an outcome. With a single event, there will be only one result, and although the shaded area result is more likely, there is no guarantee there will be a result corresponding to the shaded area.

When we work with a stream of events, we observe something else—the probability number starts describing how frequently the desired outcome occurs. It is now almost guaranteed that the desired outcome will happen—we just don't know how many times exactly. As the number of events gets bigger, the guarantee becomes stronger, and so does the likelihood of the actual number of successful outcomes being closer to the probability number. See Figure 3-2.

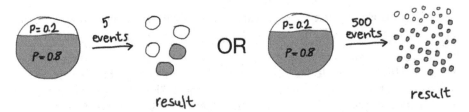

Figure 3-2. At 5 events the actual number of gray dots might not represent 80% of the total. At 500 events the actual number of gray dots is very close to 80% of the total.

When we apply a probability number on multiple independent events, things line up to what is known as normal distribution curve. It is a line that describes the likelihood of things happening as we move along a range of probable states.

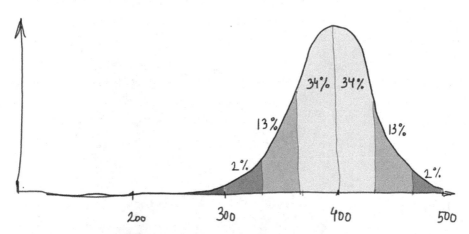

Figure 3-3. If we ran 1000 independent experiments with P=0.8 for an outcome, and with 500 samples in each experiment, and if we measure the actual number of desired outcomes per experiment, we would have a result similar to this graph. In 68% of the cases, the number of desired outcomes will be between 370 and 430, and in 95% the number will be between 330 and 470.

In a normal distribution, the most likely outcome is called "mode" (400 is the mode in Figure 3-3). Almost all, 99.6%, of the possible outcomes fall within the ±3 standard deviations from the mode. A standard deviation is a span on the dimension of interest, which span helps statisticians discuss the probability distribution easier. Each shaded area in Figure 3-3 is one standard deviation wide. Approximately 70% of all outcomes fall within ±1 standard deviation from the mode, and approximately 95% fall within ±2 standard deviations from the mode. These numbers might seem contrived, but it turns out they apply over a very large set of natural phenomena.

Let's say we have a team of two developers and have estimated (guessed) a project at 1.5 years. Let's say we have information to think that the absolute best we can do is 1 year, and based on other assumptions, we think that 2.5 years is the worst we can do. We can build a cumulative probability curve (Figure 3-4) describing how likely the estimates seem based on what we know at this moment.

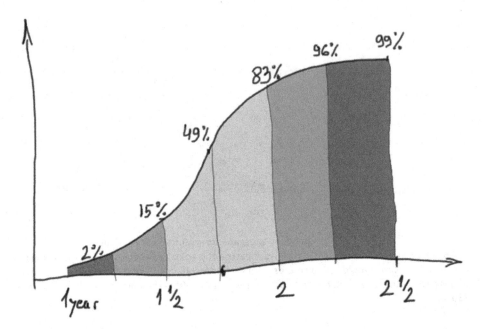

Figure 3-4. Cumulative distribution curve showing that the original 1.5-year estimate is not as likely as we might have thought when making it

The cumulative distribution curve indicates with about 85% probability that the project will be less than 2 years, and with only 15% that it will be less than the estimate of 1.5 years. Even with a grossly oversimplified model like this, we can start making some crude decisions and we can improve communications on the project.

Getting Accurate Information Based on Imprecise Inputs

The Central Limit Theorem tells us that the sum of many random and independent variables is approximately normally distributed regardless of the specific distributions of the variables. This is of great significance and is a powerful tool we can use for project planning, because projects are such a sum of large number of variables. True, they are not always independent, and they are not always completely random, but it is a good enough approximation that we can use to bypass hefty sets of complexities.

With the help of this theorem, we can view the whole project as a single (sum total) variable, and we can analyze the probability of this variable being within a certain range through the help of a normal distribution curve. Something we've been intuitively doing before, but not taking it to its logical conclusion.

What this means for us, as software developers and project managers, is that even if we botch the accuracy on every individual estimate, we can still have confidence that the sum total remains within the same normal distribution. Figure 3-5 shows that we can reason about the distribution of the sum total and make intelligent speculations for the "total accuracy" without having to worry about the accuracy of each of its elements.

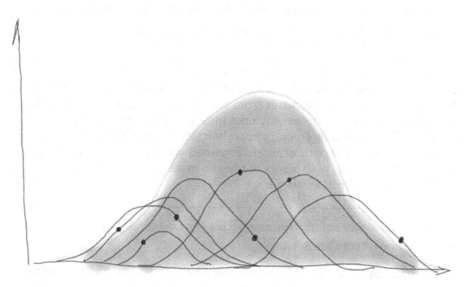

Figure 3-5. A sum total normal distribution curve comprised of multiple variables' distributions

ACCURATE ESTIMATION! WHAT IS THIS?

We should mention here that the idea of an accurate software estimate is somewhat of a misnomer. This is because the thing we are building does not exist yet. If we were to estimate the length of a ship, both the real length and the estimated value exist at the same moment in time. They can be compared and we can determine the estimation accuracy. However, if we are to estimate the effort for building something, it is only the estimation value that exists at that moment—the actual effort for building it does not exist yet and cannot be measured. Thus we don't have a reference for establishing the accuracy of our estimate.

It might be better to say "adequate estimate." However, I'll still use the notion of accuracy since it is more crisp and everyone understands what we are talking about—namely, whether the effort that we eventually expand ends up matching our original guess. But we need to recognize that there is a big time span between these two numbers being available, and we normally don't just sit and wait to see if they end up similar, but we actively apply controls to drive the project where we want it to go.

What is now left, in order to feel confident in the actual values represented by the distribution model, is finding out how much the normal distribution for the estimated effort is offset from the "real" effort. And for this, there is nothing else we can do except take measurements from reality. We can have a sufficient measurement sample within a few weekly iterations, or within 1–2 months' worth of work. Provided we work on a decently sized project, this leaves us with plenty of time to make decisions and take actions based on the information we get.

The ideal project size (for statistical forecasting) is one with more than 5–10 developers and an expected duration of more than 8–9 months.

We'll consider a project as acceptably sized when there are at least 2–3 programmers, and the initial estimate is at least 5–6 months. Forecasting for smaller projects becomes less useful, but see "Short-term estimates are not useless either" in Chapter 6.

With this knowledge we can provide accurate information for the total based on multiple inputs, each of which is inaccurate. Sometimes clients and managers expect that we nail down each software module we work on and that we expand exactly the amount of effort we estimated.

We could be working on the second module, out of a 20-module system, and it might have been estimated at 5 calendar weeks. It is now taking 7 weeks. Clients or managers might escalate the situation disproportionately. When this happens we need to remind them that we are only forecasting and managing the project, and that we do not have bandwidth (or a reason) to control the execution of each discrete module with the same precision.

Control, Lack of Control, and Precision

The statistical controls we are discussing here can be rather loose when there is a low number of sample variables on which to model the distribution. For example, if we have only delivered 3 or 4 chunks[1] from a system, and we are trying to use the available information to forecast the remaining 97 chunks, then we cannot apply statistical controls yet. Our decisions will be poorly informed. We need to work with a sample of at least 20–30 variables, and ideally more than 50, before statistical principles start to work reliably for us.

What this means in practice is that we cannot approach the management of a project purely as a statistical problem. This is because usually there are not enough chunks to get to a good sample quick enough, and we need to start making decisions before we have a solid statistical model. This translates to the team and the project manager still having to work out problems quickly and persistently, just like they would regardless of any project management techniques. For example (See Figure 3-6), if a set of functionality was estimated between 2 and 3 days and we sense trouble on day 2, we need to act[2] and not merely observe and record (for the sake of statistics) how long the job will take. We will talk about sample size later, but when the whole project scope is represented by 150–200 chunks, and we need a reasonably good forecast by the first few iterations, we need to stay firmly on the project controls from day 1.

---

[1] A chunk can be of any size and is not the same as a user story or a functional specification. A chunk represents a set of functionality which we have decided to estimate together. We will talk about resolution and splitting the whole scope in chunks later. For a large project, a single chunk can represent 3–4 weeks' worth of work for a single person or a programming pair, and for smaller projects a chunk can comprise 4–5 days' worth of work.

[2] To "act" here means to make it easier for developers to carry out the implementation work. Acting does not mean to pressure developers into speeding up—this is a useless activity from the point of view this book is taking. A scrum master or project manager can help by getting business people to prioritize the work in advance, or by working with PO (Product Owner) or BA (Business Analyst) to simplify existing specifications and requirements, or by getting coffee and cookies, and so on. A developer can help by seeking help or offering help, providing quick feedback, and so on. This is what is meant by "to act." Everyone should be working together to accomplish activities which help the team move forward expeditiously.

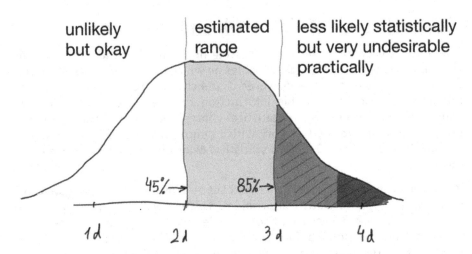

Figure 3-6. We do not want to casually venture outside of the estimation range, although statistically the event is representative of the same distribution curve

If we keep too loose control over the execution of the work, and we approach the problem as a purely statistical observation, then we can go through some large deviations from the "plan." This will make the people who are following the progress of the project uncomfortable. When people are not comfortable, it is difficult for them to trust us, and valuable energy might get expanded toward unnecessary problem solving. And even if the forecast works out well by the final stages of the project, we would have still missed the point, since it was to create trust during the project, not to prove that a conceptual model has been correct as the project is finishing.

On the other hand, if we have a knee jerk reaction on every deviation from estimates, this does not contribute to project control either. For example, if a task that was estimated at 2 days is taking a day longer (150% already), but developers know exactly why, then we should not start bothering other people with escalations or requests for help. This would only make everyone more uneasy than if we were too loose on the controls.

Overreacting can be not only useless but outright dangerous. It may destabilize the project's ecosystem to the point where things get out of the Central Limit Theorem's domain. If we alienate developers, and make people unwilling to invest their full selves into the project, we might have introduced instability that cannot work itself out by mere statistics.

The Central Limit Theorem tightens as we reach farther. The larger the project, the more useful the Central Limit Theorem becomes for practical application. This is somewhat counterintuitive but extremely important—forecasting and controlling for a long project is more manageable than for a small project. (However, guessing is more manageable for a small project.)

We still need to work out the immediate problems even on longer projects, and there will be more of those problems because of the longer timeline. But when applying project controls based on surveying longer-term goals, we can make fine input adjustments with larger impact and stay ahead of the (probable) events.

Figure 3-7 shows that at the same desired burn-up rate, and the same deviation at month 2, we need a much smaller rate adjustment on a 9-month-long project in order to compensate for the lateness, compared to the adjustment we need on a 4-month project.

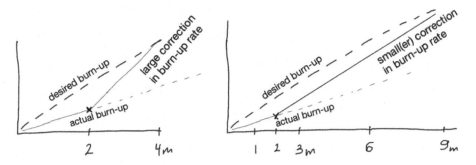

Figure 3-7. Corrective adjustment on shorter vs. longer project

Summary

Many people in the software industry, especially people working with agile software development methods, have given up on estimation and they feel it is useless. They feel it cannot be done with accuracy, or that it doesn't make a difference how precise you try to be… at the end the project is never on time. The value of a forecast for facilitating project control is being lost because of an irrelevant focus on estimation accuracy. The unwillingness of people to commit to an objective in the face of uncertainty is a direct cause of this confusion of the main purpose of a forecast. This is a mistake that ends up costing companies multimillion dollar opportunities and ruining the chances for good relationships.

Instead of forcing unneeded expectation on the precision of the initial estimation, we need to learn how to harness imprecisions and proven statistical principles, along with the capabilities and skill of our teams, in order to gain valuable business advantage. By doing this we can commit to success early, based on minimal set of data. We are not committing to a number, rather we are committing to working out an adequate and timely solution within an agreed-upon project envelope. By inverting the order of events, and agreeing to commit before we have a precise outlook, we open the possibility for a meaningful forecast, which in turn gives us the required leverage over powerful project control tools—including negotiating scope, reinventing business ideas, adjusting team composition in timely manner, and even reframing the project itself (with everyone on board).

Forecasting Mechanics

Let's get to it!

How do we put all this in practice and work out the project envelope? What exactly are the things we do to apply intelligent project control? How do we provide a clear indication of progress, maintain the required team workload throughout the project, and allow business people and the delivery team ample time for scope considerations and decisions? How can we do something today that helps us aim at a 2-week time window 12 months in the future?

The method for intelligent forecasting is a practical application of the scientific method and can be broken down in the following steps:

1. Define a scale (ballpark approximation)—Scale can be as wide as the expected project length or it can be some portion of it. It is not to be confused with an overall estimate of the project. It might be roughly similar in length, but the actual project estimate is produced later.

2. Define a resolution—Resolution represents the number of chunks in which we need to break up work in order to gain a sufficient statistical grip. Higher resolution provides an increased certainty, but it also costs progressively more to sustain.

D. Dimitrov, *Software Project Estimation*,
https://doi.org/10.1007/978-1-4842-5025-9_5

3. Initial estimation and sizing—Based on the desired resolution and other factors, we need to design ranges for estimating effort. Once we go through the initial estimation, we can size the project and take a first guess at whether the team has enough capacity.

4. Adjust for calendar time—It is crucial to convert the effort estimates into calendar time. This is because the actual completion data we collect in the next step is based on calendar time. Once we convert effort estimation into calendar times, we can also speculate about optimistic and pessimistic completion dates for the project.

5. Collect data—Estimation data is only one input for the forecast. Tracking the actual implementation times and observing other contextual factors provide another set of input information. The relationship between estimates and actual completion times becomes the basis for adjustments and predictive accuracy.

6. Identify trends and scenarios—Once we have collected enough data, we can start analyzing, making projections, and evaluating different scenarios.

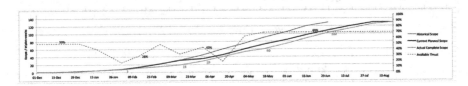

Figure 4-1. A chart depicting project burn-up along with the team's available thrust

Figure 4-1 shows an example output of this process. This chart captures the evolution of the project delivery, and when used in the early months of a project can facilitate the decision making needed for applying confident project management.

We will discuss and reveal the elements of this and a few other charts throughout the remainder of the book. In this chapter we focus on the mechanics of obtaining a meaningful forecast—diagramming, defining suitable chart scale, partitioning the scope to facilitate estimation, sizing the project, collecting data, and producing a plot on the chart. In the next chapter, we will analyze various chart indications and discuss the project controls that we can apply.

The discussion in this chapter moves much closer to the practical application of the estimation method. For those readers who enjoy spreadsheet formulas and charts, the sample spreadsheets and diagrams in Appendix B at the end of the book and at www.apress.com/9781484250242 might facilitate your familiarization with the details of the method further.

Determining the Chart Area

The scale/ballpark. The first thing to do when building a forecasting model is to prepare the "charting surface" by figuring out the rough scale of the effort. What we come up with at this point is not an estimate. It is only an idea of the scale at which we want to be working. Is it a few months, a year, or more? This choice is very important for the utility of the resulting forecast. If the scale is too large, we might not be able to pick up on important project events, and if the scale is too small, we might not be able to anticipate far enough.

In Figure 4-2 we can see two different approaches for selecting a forecast chart scale. An approximately 1:1 ratio scale is selected for the project with an expected length of 11 months on the left and a 1:3 scale for the 24-month project on the right.

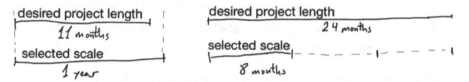

Figure 4-2. Selecting an adequate forecasting scale

It is important not to confuse the scale with an estimate or a forecast. At this point we are only figuring out a number (time period) which will help us build a meaningful chart—one that will help us with its indications. The selection is not unlike choosing the right scale for a driving map, where a city map will have a large scale, a country map a medium scale, and a continent map a small scale.

Resolution. I define resolution as the number of chunks we want to work with for a given scale. You might have seen it elsewhere as sample size. Higher resolution provides for a more controlled application of the statistical principles on which this method relies. However, having too high of a resolution adds more noise than valuable information, and it also costs more than the utility it brings. Having too low of a resolution makes the forecast loose and less useful for promoting trust. We need to find pragmatic resolution and work within this "normal" range.

Statistics starts being applicable once there are at least 30 samples. At this resolution the confidence levels from statistical analysis are relatively low. At a resolution of 60–70, we can get to statistical error of 15%. At 200–300 variables, the expected error goes down to about 5%. At a set of 2000 variables, the statistical error can drop to less than 3%.

In software development, aiming for early forecast precision of 5% is naive at best and unethical if done by people with experience. If the project sponsors are calculating their business opportunities at precision levels of 5%, then something is seriously wrong. Early confidence of between 5% and 10% is extremely challenging in software development, and a confidence between 10% and 15% should be sufficient for anyone with a practical business need. Business people should be able to maneuver within this range of uncertainty and make useful business decisions without putting undue administrative stress on a project.

CONFIDENCE LEVELS

You might have seen the "Cone of Uncertainty" diagram that depicts how confidence levels get progressively better as a waterfall project moves along the phases of initial concept, approved product definition, requirements complete, user interface design complete, detailed specification design complete, and so on. You may have noticed that the estimation error at the start of development phase is 10–15%.

The difference here is that not all "15%" are equal. The 10–15% we are discussing in this book are based on data and statistics. The 10–15% people mentioned in "traditional" estimation approaches are based on a belief, such as "I believe that the accuracy of this estimate is 10%. It has to be, we spent a lot of time on it and estimated based on very detailed specifications. I mean, it has to be 10% or better. Worst case scenario it's 15%, but not more."

Therefore, a useful and pragmatic resolution level is around 100 samples on the lower end, and 250–300 on the higher end. Keep in mind that we are not leaving the fate of a project in the hands of chance and statistics alone. We are applying active project control based on multiple inputs, with the forecast being only one of them.

Imagine we are one and a half months into a year-long project (i.e., there are a little more than 10 months left). The following statements ought to be sufficient for an intelligent follow-up conversations and decision making:

- "We are 80% confident that with the current team setup we need 2 months longer than the current plan."

- "We are 80% confident that we need 3 more people with compatible skills to join the team within the next 1 month if we are to make the original deadline."

- "We are 80% confident that unless we cut functionality in these three specific modules, we cannot make the timeline with the current setup of the team."

If people are able to start this type of conversations less than 2 months into a 1-year-long project, and their confidence levels are (meaningful) 80% or 90%, then this is all that is needed—a trustworthy method for pulling problem solving early into the project. When we pull problems early, the proposed solutions have an improved chance of positively affecting the outcome. And we might even have time for additional solutioning, should the selected approaches prove ineffective within a reasonable timeframe.

PLAN-DO-CHECK-ACT

The essence of project control is *observe, think, act, observe* (Figure 4-3). It is a variation of the PDCA cycle (Plan-Do-Check-Act) of many continuous processes. The essence of project management, and its associated practices, is to secure the environment where this type of control is feasible.

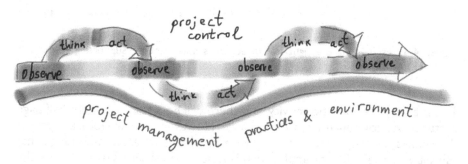

Figure 4-3. PDCA model for project control and the accompanying project management practices

Sizing the Project

Estimation ranges. We need to break down the scope into desired resolution. Whether we have a large system specification document or we are just starting with identifying a story map, we need to comprehend the known project scope. Splitting the known scope into the necessary number of chunks to support the resolution is relatively straightforward. In order to facilitate this process, it's worth identifying meaningfully sized buckets (see Figure 4-4) that developers can use for labeling the chunks of work.

The proposed software solution needs to be captured in the form of a specification. It is irrelevant whether we've done this through a specification document, a story map, or a flat backlog of stories and epics. The important thing is that some areas of the solution are described in enough detail to be broken down in meaningful chunks.

For example, if we have a specification of 100 pages and the level of detail is relatively consistent throughout the document, then we can assume that half a page will contain enough material so that we can split the app in 200 chunks. Similarly, if we have a story map, we can figure out a way to chunk it even when some of the stories are not detailed yet.

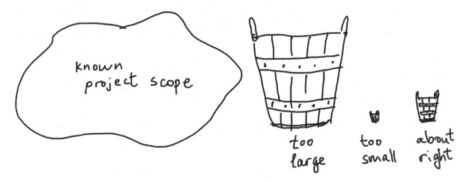

Figure 4-4. Establishing the right size of bucket is important for supporting a workable resolution

This is a very mechanistic activity, and there will be instances where half page captures way too much work or too little. However, once we look at a few of the chunks, we can start getting a sense of what is an estimation range that can support them. For example, we might be working on a system where the first few chunks all feel between 1 and 3 weeks' worth of effort. We can then design two ranges from 1 to 1.5 weeks and from 1.2 to 2.5 weeks and proceed with fitting the rest of the chunks using these two ranges. When we stumble on an area of the system with insufficient detail, we can define large and extra-large ranges to support whatever chunks we can carve out.

T-shirt sizing is ideal for this and we can choose to have five ranges when there is more variation in detail (XS, S, M, L, XL), or only three ranges (S, M, L) when the detail is more consistent (see Figure 4-5).

Figure 4-5. Some of the buckets (S, M) support the desired resolution better, but we should provide smaller and larger buckets just in case some of the chunks are not the "ideal" size

The estimation ranges are in "days' worth of effort" and not calendar time. With an average chunk size of between 1 and 2.5 weeks (supporting the desired resolution), we might have these ranges:

XS = less than 5 days (less than 1 week)

S = 4 to 7 days (0.8 weeks to 1.4 weeks)

M = 6 to 12 days (1.2 weeks to 2.4 weeks)

L= 10 to 19 days (2 weeks to 3.8 weeks)

XL = 16 to 30 days (3.2 to 6 weeks)

On a smaller project, we might have smaller ranges supporting the same resolution:

XS = less than 0.8 days

S = 0.5 to 1.5 days

M = 1.3 to 2.5 days

L = 1.8 to 4 days

XL = 3.5 to 6 days

I try to gauge it so that the S and M ranges are around or slightly smaller than the average chunk size. This way, when most chunks fall within these two ranges, we should end up with a total number of chunks that is around or slightly larger than the target resolution.

Establishing the initial estimation ranges is best done if the ranges are slightly overlapping and progressively growing (see Figure 4-6). A tighter range selection, without excessive overlap, creates a slight pressure for developers so they don't accidentally stop paying attention when throwing chunks into the buckets. Too little or no overlap generates the wrong type of pressure—chunks which estimate seems close to the upper limit of a range will routinely be labeled as belonging to the next larger range for safety. I like the end limits oscillating around the Fibonacci numbers and the ranges overlapping at about 20–30% of the smaller range. The other thing to look for is to make the largest range not much larger than two times the chunk size supporting the resolution.

Having five ranges is preferred because it lets the developers feel unobstructed, and it makes for a quicker exercise. But three ranges will work too. The overlap is important because it puts developers at ease. They see right away that a chunk can go one way or another, and they appreciate this flexibility since it properly reflects their real experiences with estimation. They are willing to not overestimate, because they realize the next chunk might go the other way too.

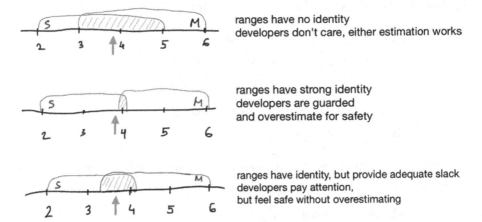

Figure 4-6. The gray arrow indicates what is the "gut feel" of developers—a little more than 3 ½ but less than 4. Ranges with no identity are less useful in subsequent forecasting. Ranges with strong identity trigger developers to overestimate. Developers are inclined to label the story as M more often in the second example than in the third example. (The numbers here might represent days' worth of work, or weeks' worth of work.)

With properly sized ranges, people get into collaborative mode much sooner, and estimates for large sets of functionality get done quickly. It almost becomes a game. In contrast, when the ranges are not overlapping, or if developers are forced to estimate with "precision" (in exact hours, and not in ranges), they are much more cautious what estimate to assign, and this leads to routine overestimation, frustration, and lengthy argumentations, which cost significant time, bring no value, and ruin the relationships within the team.

Estimating the work. Now that we have the estimation ranges defined, we need to break the known scope of work into pieces and start estimating. We estimate in days' worth of effort per single track,[1] that is, if the developers had the day exclusively for delivering working software—programming, designing, and testing. If we observe that most chunks get in the S and M buckets, then we can just keep going. Some pieces will end up being XS, and some will end up L or even XL, but the bulk of the pieces should be in the S and M ranges (see Figure 4-7).

Figure 4-7. Aim to have chunks split in a way that makes them suitable for the S and M buckets. It is okay to have a few spill over into the other buckets. (Do you notice the normal distribution?)

If too many pieces end up in the L and XL buckets (and if it looks like we won't get enough chunks to get to the desired resolution), then we need to split those chunks further so we get them down to S or M. If most of the pieces get estimated as XS, then we need to zoom out and look at less detail. This is where a good business analyst or a product owner can provide just enough detail so the developers can split or aggregate the work. And a scrum master or project manager can keep the process moving quickly, helping people zoom in or out as needed so they don't get stuck on irrelevant debates.

The one thing we don't want to do at this step of the process is to burden developers with a request for precision estimates just because there is a detailed specification (see Figure 4-8). People might argue that a developer

---

[1] Sometimes a track might be a small team. I worked on a project where two programmers would couple with a single tester. The three developers would be working almost exclusively together. On that project we estimated the functionality that the whole trio could complete in a day/week worth of work. Two such mini-teams were working on a single track of functionality. We had three tracks at the peak.

should be able to gauge the effort with precision if the functionality is described with great detail. But it doesn't work that way in software development. The specification detail doesn't provide developers much help for estimating a piece of work with higher accuracy. However, detailed specification helps for breaking the work into smaller chunks. The smaller chunks can then be estimated at a higher resolution. If we want better accuracy for the final forecast, we need to aim for a higher resolution, and not for higher accuracy of individual estimates. The objective of the T-shirt sizing exercise is to get as many chunks as we need estimated and get it over with quickly.

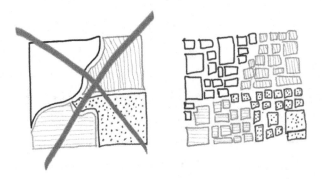

Figure 4-8. Do not ask developers to provide high precision estimates for intricate functionality based on detailed specification. Ask them to provide high resolution estimates even if each individual estimate is of lower accuracy.

Estimating at a very high resolution is wasteful. We need to pay the cost of business analysts and developers looking at too many details and scrum masters or project managers having to track too many pieces of data. It can slightly speed up the forecasting when we start collecting data, and it can provide a (false) sense of certainty, but it costs more than the value it contributes. We should work at a resolution that makes sense and be careful every time we lead people into thinking we are working at too fine of a precision. Most likely we cannot achieve that precision for the final forecast,[2] and no one needs it—people only need an adequate guidance toward the objective.

---

[2] I worked with a new CTO some time ago and he announced that we were going to start estimating and delivering all projects with a precision of +/- 1 day. He was reasoning that if the airlines are able to schedule transcontinental flights with precision of minutes, we should be able to deliver 3–4-month-long projects with a precision of 1 day. The frequency of deployment to production was once every three weeks because of dependencies with marketing campaigns and with other departments. Even if we were able to forecast within 1 day of the actual delivery, it would bring small practical value.

If the developers cannot engage in the kind of estimates discussed earlier, but the product owner or business analyst believes there is sufficient specification detail, we as scrum masters or project managers need to make sure developers understand that the result of this estimation is only one of the inputs for the forecast. It is not a binding contract or a final commitment. Their responsibility is to make a fair attempt at guessing the amount of work needed for each chunk and to be consistent, so that if two pieces of work seem equal in size, they get estimated approximately the same. Developers should definitely not throw random estimates, as this will sabotage the exercise and possibly the project.

First stab at planning. If you haven't cringed at some of the simplifications so far, you might get a cringe now. However, before we go through this, let's state one more time that the purpose of estimation and early planning is to enable intelligent project control through the rest of the project. The purpose is not to produce an accurate and precise guess at the beginning of the project.

Suppose we want to finish the project in 12 months and we have estimated all the work as if a pair of programmers will be working on it. Let's say that when we sum all the estimations, we get 3 years' worth of effort.

Figure 4-9. In a single track, the whole project is delivered one bucket at a time

If we only had these two developers (see Figure 4-9), then there is obviously no way to complete the project in 1 year. There are certainly things we can discuss with business people and choose a meaningful 1-year goal. But if we want to finish the whole project in 1 year, then we need a larger team. The mechanistic "mythical man-month" approach is to simply figure out how many tracks are needed to complete the project (see Figure 4-10).

Figure 4-10. In a multitrack, the project is delivered a few buckets at a time. Thus the work gets complete quicker

However, there are software development laws[3] that prohibit this rectangular approach. Gall's Law in particular says that we cannot start with a complex team. In practice this means that we should start with a single track effort until the solution and the team has matured enough to sustain two tracks. After some period the team and the solution might graduate to three, four, or more simultaneous tracks.

The problem becomes to allow ample time for team growth while supporting the completion of the project within the desired timeframe. The large things to consider are people's skill, team's autonomy for technical decisions, team compatibility (self-selection?), collocation or lack of, and effort time vs. calendar time.

First pass project projection. We just stated that the estimation based on the initial XS, S, M, L, and XL ranges is not contractual—there is no immediate commitment. But business people often need an early idea for the expected size of the effort before they commence. What can we do? We can produce a range. In this case we can build a range from an optimistic and pessimistic prognosis for the required effort.

You cannot undercommunicate the fact that this will only be a guess. People should treat it that way. Make sure that if any of the numbers and dates gets picked as project targets, people realize these are the aspirational targets we want or hope to meet, not the targets we have promised we will meet.

---

[3] See Appendix A for more information about software development laws.

RELATIVE ESTIMATION

Beware of the relative estimation technique that is discussed in many books on agile software development. It looks something like Figure 4-11, and the accompanying description usually says that a "stone" that looks twice the size of another "stone" is twice as big. However, this is not true. A stone that looks twice as big as another stone will be eight times larger, because a stone is three dimensional, and two raised to the third power is eight ($2^3 = 8$). In software, the work is often multidimensional and the effect of this visual "illusion" can be even larger. (Some of the typical dimensions are business rules, software architecture and design, database access, performance, security, usability, accessibility, visual design, automation and documentation, training.)

Figure 4-11. Relative estimation

When initially estimating the chunks of work for the whole project, we would do better if we looked at each one separately and give it our best shot of placing it in the right bucket, without comparing it too much with chunks we have already estimated. This way we don't inadvertently compound the estimation "errors."

> The technique of relative sizing is adequate when applied on an iteration
> level estimation in "story points," because at that time developers are
> intimately familiar with the context. Story points are not useful for initial
> project estimation and forecasting, but they serve a different and very
> important role. We will talk about it later in this chapter.

We can add up all the lower limits of the chunks' ranges, and all the upper
limits. This way we can come up with two numbers, each unlikely, but
encompassing the likely scenarios (see Figure 4-12). Again, a range is a useful
simplification when we are trying to work with complex problems without
the benefit of having experienced all the complexities yet.

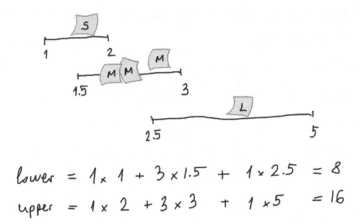

$$lower = 1 \times 1 + 3 \times 1.5 + 1 \times 2.5 = 8$$
$$upper = 1 \times 2 + 3 \times 3 + 1 \times 5 = 16$$

Figure 4-12. We can calculate the lower and upper estimation limits for the whole project
by summing the lower and upper range limits of all pieces. The numbers here can be days',
weeks', or months' worth of effort.

Keep in mind that this is the implementation effort. For *duration* range we
need to adjust for calendar time.

Adjusting for calendar time. It is wise to not confuse effort estimates
with calendar time. Such confusion is a naive mistake, but sometimes people
do it when rushed to produce a convenient answer. When we ask developers
whether something takes 2–3 days, we are really asking whether it is 2–3 days
of implementation work (a.k.a. programming), not whether it is 2–3 days on
the calendar. If developers need to attend meetings for 3–4 hours a day, the
effective time for implementation work becomes 2 hours per day, and a piece
of work estimated at 2–3 days might take 8–12 days on the calendar, that is,
2–3 weeks.

One way to translate between effort and calendar time is to add certain buffers that make sense in the particular situation. Meeting time is only one of the things we need to consider when converting effort estimates to calendar time. On a longer project, people need to take vacation, which might be up to 10% of the calendar time. We can apply this buffer without asking people for actual vacation plans.[4] There are many other activities that do not directly contribute to software. (There is a longer discussion on this type of safety buffers in the "Navigating Issues" section of Chapter 6.)

Multiplying the optimistic and pessimistic end of the effort range by 1.5 might be an honest thing to do when converting to calendar time as long as we can explain what goes into the extra 0.5 (50%) that we are factoring in. We can also produce a "realistic" estimate by using PERT calculation (see Figure 4-13), or by locating a point reasonably spaced between the optimistic and pessimistic limits.

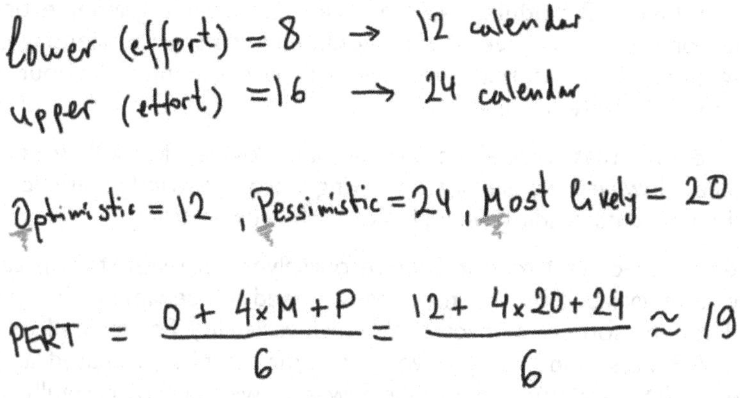

$$\text{lower (effort)} = 8 \rightarrow 12 \text{ calendar}$$

$$\text{upper (effort)} = 16 \rightarrow 24 \text{ calendar}$$

$$\text{Optimistic} = 12, \text{Pessimistic} = 24, \text{Most lively} = 20$$

$$\text{PERT} = \frac{O + 4 \times M + P}{6} = \frac{12 + 4 \times 20 + 24}{6} \approx 19$$

Figure 4-13. PERT formula for realistic estimate is E = (O + 4xM + P)/6, where O is optimistic, M is most likely, and P is a pessimistic prognosis. (The effort-to-calendar conversion ratio is 1.5.)

Again, tell people this is only where we are aiming, not where we are going. At least not yet.

Fine-tuning. The problem with coarse breakdown is that we need a longer period to start getting meaningful data, and if managers and business people are tingling for an outlook, this will make them nervous. The problem with too fine breakdown is that it becomes an impossible work to manage when the project is larger. A viable approach is to break down the whole project

---

[4] Treating people with respect should be considered a project control. By planning around people's needs instead of having people adjust their needs according to a forced plan, we improve the chances for a wholehearted commitment throughout the duration of the project.

coarsely, and then to break down the "first phase" of the project in fine-grained chunks. This way we can start getting meaningful data quickly at the fine-grained level. As time goes by, we will start getting meaningful data on the coarse level (project level) as well, but we would have not starved people who need forecasting data sooner (whether for comfort or otherwise).

For large projects we should set fine-tuned T-shirt ranges for the first one or two phases and have a coarse T-shirt size for the whole project. Let's say we are working on a system that consists of 18 modules of similar complexity. We can split each module in 7–10 chunks and measure those against the coarse T-shirt size on the project level.

We can then break the first 3 modules in about 30 pieces each, and size these chunks against the fine-grained T-shirt ranges for the first "phase." As we move through the first 30 or so fine-grained pieces, we can roughly see if the plan for the first 3 modules is coming along. Later, as we are getting ready with the first 3 modules, we can decide if more fine-grained estimation is needed or if we now have enough confidence to start projecting on the coarse-grained data. At that time we will have completed about 20–30 chunks on the coarse level.

Earlier, we said that a 20–30-piece sample provides for a low statistical confidence. However, we are not observing a project strictly statistically, nor is this the only data reading we will take at the coarse level.

We need to be careful to not deceive ourselves with statistics in case we observe large variability. If this happens, we need to reexamine the approach and look for the source of unacceptably high variability. For example, if the M range is 2–3 days, and we observe that some chunks estimated as M get delivered in 0.5 days, but others take 2 weeks, we need to carefully look at the details. If these happen sporadically, we might be okay without corrective action.

OPERATE AT THE RIGHT LEVEL

If the data from the coarse-level tracking and forecasting is telling us that things are not going well, do not attempt to discover a solution for the problems by diving into fine-grained estimation and tracking. Getting tight control on smaller-scale issues will not provide enough project control to recover from larger problems that are already affecting the project.

Plotting a Dot

Mapping. Mapping out the actual implementation data to the initial estimation is the most laborious part of the work. Some project management tools might be able to help, but a simple spreadsheet should be enough.

Let's say we have a chunk of work estimated as size M and that this means 2–3 weeks at the set resolution. Once we started the implementation work, this chunk of functionality had to be broken down into multiple stories (or tasks, work items, etc.). We need to figure out which stories belong to which chunk of the original breakdown. This can be facilitated by keeping things well organized and labeled (see Figure 4-14). A tool like Jira can help with the labeling/tagging feature. It is important to not confuse chunks with epics.

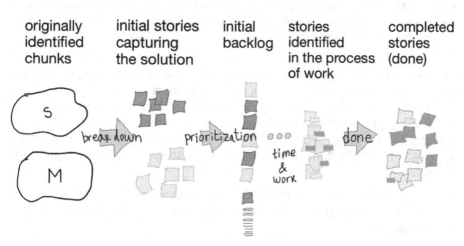

| originally identified chunks | initial stories capturing the solution | initial backlog | stories identified in the process of work | completed stories (done) |

Figure 4-14. The challenge with mapping is to properly map the stories that appeared in the process of work back to the originally estimated chunks of scope. Notice the small labels in the "stories identified in the process of work" column. If we have missed tagging the stories appropriately at the time of their origination, then we need to backtrack and figure out which area of the solution they belong to.

Once we have mapped the completed stories/tasks back to the originally estimated chunks, the product owner needs to assess the level of completeness of each chunk that has some complete work mapped to it (see Figure 4-15). If we have completed three stories against a chunk sized as M, the product owner might feel that 80% of the functionality is covered, or he/she may feel it's only 40%.

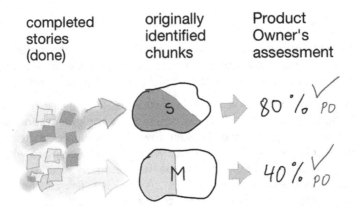

Figure 4-15. The product owner needs to assess what percentage of the desired solution (represented by the originally identified chunks) is covered by the demonstrated and working functionality of the completed stories

Whether the mapping is trivial or demanding, we should approach it with patience and an open mind. It might take a few hours or even a day, but it is a few hours well spent, and it might also help with learning more about the state of the project. Items we thought were done might turn out to be only half done, and things we thought were scheduled for next release might appear only partially done. It is an opportunity to spot details we might have missed.

Plotting. With all this work out of the way, we can now "calculate" the scope we have covered (Figure 4-16). We are ready to plot the first dot on the forecast graph.

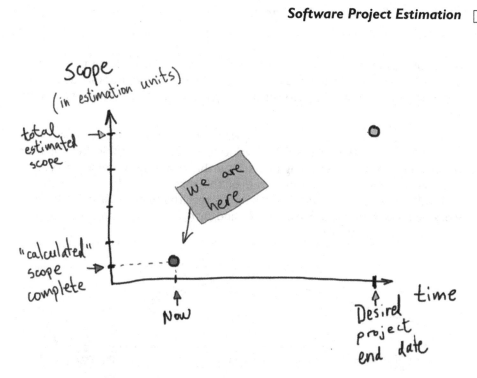

Figure 4-16. The first data-driven indication on the forecast is applied against the calculated completed scope. The desired project end date and the total estimated scope define two of the project envelope limits at this moment.

Don't let the crude form of this graph fool you. Its data-driven aspect more than compensates for the small imperfections of a manual drawing. We know where we have started, we know where we are now, and we know where we want to go. We are getting closer to being able to forecast.

The Other Two Pillars

The Central Limit Theorem works very well for the application described so far. But it is not sufficient by itself. There are two other crucially important principles that must be satisfied for us to be able to forecast intelligently. They are "Sustainable pace of work" and "Done."

Sustainable pace of work. We often see software development teams, who work in an agile style, estimating user stories in story points. The number of points delivered within an iteration is called velocity. Story points and velocity don't relate directly to the estimation or forecasting for the whole project. One reason for this is that they change meaning throughout the project, as they are affected by what the team learns each iteration.

Another reason is that sometimes we don't have enough detail to estimate everything in points. Even if we had enough detail, it would not make sense to spend time understanding features and dependencies at the level needed for story points.

However, story points and measuring velocity are of paramount importance for the forecast's worthiness. Their value is in setting a sustainable pace for the team. A team not working in a sustainable way cannot deliver a project that can be reliably forecasted. One of the three principles on which the method of intelligent forecasting is based is that the team must be capable of working consistently (see Figure 4-17), and story points are a perfect tool for ensuring this consistency.

Figure 4-17. Statistics alone is not enough to support intelligent forecasting. The project team must be capable of sustaining an optimal pace of work throughout the duration of the project.

Sustainable pace does not necessarily mean a constant pace, as teams typically need time to reach their optimal pace. Teams can also innovate and accelerate. During innovative periods, the pace of delivery might suffer at first and then it can pick up again. There is also normal fluctuation based on the work complexity. As long as the team's productivity remains within a satisfactory bandwidth, we can consider this mode of operation sustainable (see the diagram on the left in Figure 4-18).

If there are short bursts of output followed by deep troughs of endless bug fixing (see the diagram on the right in Figure 4-18) and zero or negative architectural progress, then the team is not capable of delivering in a sustainable way.

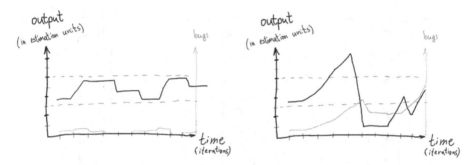

Figure 4-18. The diagram on the left shows sustainable work, and the one to the right shows unsustainable work. Even if the average output ends up relatively equal for the depicted period, the project on the right is too volatile and it is accumulating bugs, which will eventually drive it out of usable power.

Engineering techniques like automated unit testing, test-driven development (TDD), refactoring, and continuous integration and continuous delivery (CI and CD) greatly contribute toward a team's capability for sustainable work. These practices are not the domain of iterative delivery models, and if a team is practicing them proficiently, they can very likely maintain sustainable pace.

If these software delivery practices are absent, and if regression issues consume progressively larger bandwidth, we need to account for it in the forecast. Regardless of whether we use an iterative approach or we follow a big waterfall plan, we have to be honest about the team's capabilities. Deteriorating code base and regression issues can render the team's productivity to zero quickly.

Done. Done is a concept I first encountered in a formalized way when working with Scrum. So I attribute it to Scrum. Wherever it originates, probably in XP, the effect it has on our ability to intelligently forecast, plan, and manage the project is binary—that is, if we cannot work within a definition of Done,[5] we cannot intelligently plan or manage a project. "Done" is the

---

[5] Definition of Done is a set of conditions that the team determines as sufficient for guaranteeing valuable software. For a more thorough description, please see here: www.scruminc.com/definition-of-done/

third pillar to support scientific forecasting (see Figure 4-19). The project team must be capable of disciplined software delivery within desired and agreed-upon parameters.

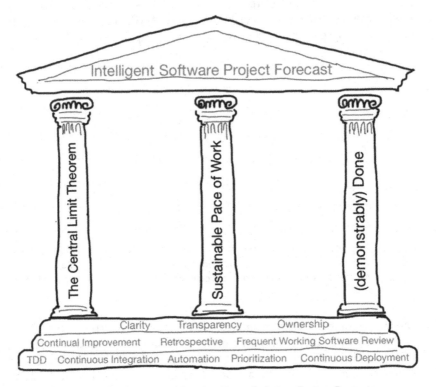

Figure 4-19. The three pillars supporting Intelligent Software Project Forecast

The definition from Scrum Inc. might be a bit overzealous, but is a good place to start contemplating on your team's capability to work within a definition of Done:

> *Done means coded to standards, reviewed, implemented with unit Test-Driven Development (TDD), tested with 100 percent test automation, integrated and documented.*

> —Scrum Inc.

If we are delivering code, but we cannot claim that a specific piece of functionality is done, then for all practical purposes we should not include the expanded effort toward the project's progress. And if none of the stories can be claimed as done, we should not claim any progress—that is, even if we labored for 2 weeks, we have to account for zero delivered scope.

When we cannot claim Done, then the useful output is imaginary. The diagram on the left in Figure 4-20 shows a project pretending to be delivering consistently, but without anyone validating that the software is Done (the dashed line is the pretend output, and the solid line at the very bottom is the real output). The bugs might be underreported since the software is not being tested or demonstrated to clients. The diagram on the right of Figure 4-20 shows a project with accumulating bugs, but people still insisting that the software is Done. Ideally people should agree to not claim Done when there are uncontrollable functionality bugs, or they will get disillusioned further into the project.

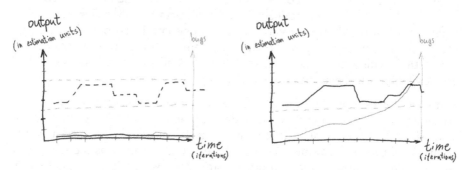

Figure 4-20. Imaginary progress—on the left code is not tested, on the right code is accepted when there are bugs

It is often the case on waterfall projects that people claim 80% readiness on some functionality, only to have this same status reported week after week without the ability to identify any single piece that is 100% done. On such projects, the assessment for completeness is expected by a developer. The 80% readiness level claimed by the developer is not suitable for forecasting, since it is not validated by a business person or a user. Project managers and business people on such dysfunctional projects usually say that they need 100% complete functionality before engaging with verifying it, thus leaving the developers in a perpetual state of uncertainty.

Please note that this is dramatically different than having small pieces of functionality claimed as 100% done and confirmed by a business person. In this case we can still say we are 80% done with a larger component of work, but it actually means that about 80% of the work toward the large component is done. We can reasonably expect to have about 20% work left. When we asked the product owner to assess the completeness levels of work items (in the mapping activity earlier), it was based on "demonstrably done" functionality, not on how many lines of code developers believe are needed before the code is done.

Working within a definition of done is more difficult on waterfall projects. This is primarily because business people wait for the hand-off at the end of the development phase. However, the technical practices of test automation and refactoring, which enable a team to work within a definition of done, are not exclusively reserved for iteratively run projects. Teams using these techniques can get very close to the benefits of working within a definition of done, even if they work on a waterfall project and cannot secure the continual interaction with business partners.

The two pillars that support predictability and confidence—"Sustainable pace of work" and "Done"—go hand in hand. If a team does not maintain sustainable pace, they will start cutting corners and step outside the definition of done; if the team does work in a sustainable pace but starts casually going out of the definition of done, then they will very soon become incapable of sustaining the pace—they will get bogged down in problems. "Done" gives us confidence about the validity of present claims, and "Sustainable pace" provides for predictability of projections.

Software delivery practices like test-driven development, automation, and continuous integration and product development practices like relentless prioritization, continuous deployment, and continual usability testing greatly facilitate a mode of operation where teams can consistently work within a definition of done and deliver at a pace which is sustainable and commercially viable.

Forecasting

We now have almost all that is needed to start forecasting. We have one data point and we have a starting (zero) point. For smaller projects with healthy teams, a satisfactory end project forecast can be generated on these two pieces of data alone. But for longer or more complex projects, it is worth plotting at least three data points before building a forecast model.

One dot on a graph is just that—a single dot. It allows us to build a linear forecast and that is rarely sufficient (see Figure 4-21). There are too many activities at the start of a project, and a straight projection line will likely skew the picture (negatively) more than we want. Two, and ideally three, readings provide for a projection that reflect the team's sustainable pace better (see Figure 4-22). Spacing the readings a few iterations apart allows for the team to reach that normal pace of development and for us, project managers and scrum masters, to forecast more meaningfully.

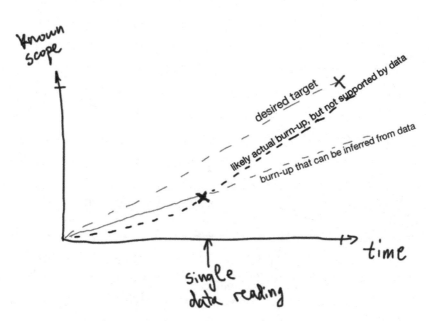

Figure 4-21. Data reading marked with "x". A single data reading is a good starting point, but it usually skews the projection negatively compared to the likely actual situation. However, on shorter projects this might be all that is needed to support decision making.

Depending on how the project is going, and how the clients feel, we might choose to go with one or more additional readings (especially if the iterations are shorter). If after a few readings we still do not feel sufficiently confident to commit to a full forecast, we should find out what information we can start communicating, because the utility of a forecast diminishes with time. Three readings close to each other provide an improved trend compared to a single reading. A reasonably spaced fourth data reading might "improve" the forecast further, but pushes the decision-making process too late into the project. An earlier decision based on less precise forecast might be preferable. Some decisions like adding additional team members only make sense when done early into a project. Later into the project, we might be left only with the options to cut scope or extend the project.

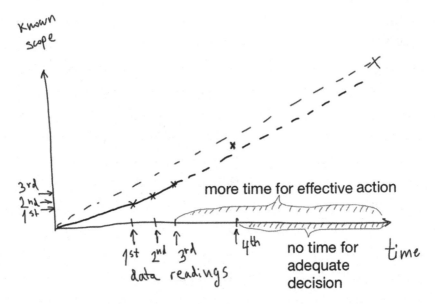

Figure 4-22. Data readings marked with "x". We forecast to make timely decisions, and an early and sufficiently grounded forecast might be more useful than a later and more precise forecast.

This method is capable of producing surprisingly stable and reliable results. It facilitates confidence and awareness, which allow business folks to make calm decisions even when faced with tough problems. Clarity, a core tenet of agile software development, is improved significantly with a reliable forecasting like this, and the positive effect on the project environment cannot be overstated.

Congratulations! You have produced the first scientific forecast for your projects. You can now enlighten business people with meaningful information. Instead of being dragged into status report meetings, the project team can now get to focus on prioritization, scope deferral, and clarifications—allowing business people to apply real project control.[6]

Summary

Modern-day software delivery techniques enable project forecasting in a way that was previously not feasible. Tools like unit testing, test automation, TDD (test-driven development), CI/CD (continuous integration/continuous deployment), refactoring, and source control and practices like 40-hour

---

[6] As opposed to the artificial control people attempt to apply when escalating issues and amplifying the pressure days before deadlines.

workweek, short iterative software delivery, continual improvement through retrospectives, and continual user review of working software enable teams to deliver with reliability that was rarely attainable in the past. This makes forecasting on the vast majority of software projects not only possible but quite reliable and inexpensive, thus providing business people with a meaningful project outlook.

By investing a few hours of work in producing intelligent project data, we can significantly improve the environment on the project for everyone. *Manifesto for Agile Software Development* is about building software. Yet, the principles of the manifesto are fairly applicable in a broad general context. The very first postulate of the manifesto is "Individuals and interactions over processes and tools"—by supporting the individuals and their needs, we stay true to what is at the core of better ways of working.

Adjustments

In software projects, like in most situations involving human relationships, it is worth the effort to provide meaningful information to people so that they gain situational awareness and make intelligent choices. Complete awareness is of course neither possible nor needed, but a small effort can go a long way toward significant improvements and avoiding major contentions. Schedule uncertainty of 30–50% or more is likely to create unneeded pressure and turmoil on any project. Many people operate at these levels of uncertainty routinely and for long periods. On the other hand, verbally maintaining that we work at 10–15% uncertainty, without being able to support the claims with data, is as unnerving if not more so. If we can find a workable method for bringing the uncertainty level reliably to 10–15%, supported by meaningful data, it will spare the team and clients valuable energy, unnecessary worry, and loss of time.

We were already careful to not confuse effort estimate with calendar time, and we corrected the initial "plans" by tracking the actual completion times. We are now going to look at a few more adjustments to the forecasting model that will further enhance our understanding of the project's progress and the accuracy of the resulting projections.

Available Thrust

Now that we have a forecast diagram, we need to figure out how to translate the information into intelligent decisions in order to adjust the project's progress closer to the path we want. Plotting the diagram and looking at the

D. Dimitrov, *Software Project Estimation*,
https://doi.org/10.1007/978-1-4842-5025-9_6

forecast is only the observational part of the effort. Applying project control is the real purpose of this observation. Remember, once the end date of a project is near, we have very limited ability for significant improvements to the project's performance. Consequently, we want to apply adequate control as early in the project as possible. The more stabilized the project performance is in its early and mid-stages, the greater the probability of arriving at the desired destination.

I was delighted when I read that the burndown chart in Scrum is based on Jeff Sutherland's experience landing fighter jets.[1] I, too, enjoy flying and have always found flying and project management to be close in many ways. When I was developing this forecasting technique, one such important similarity that took a central spot in the model was *available thrust*. The available thrust of an airplane is the force with which the propeller or jet engine can push the airplane forward (kind of). The available thrust determines the maximum angle of climb the airplane can perform. There are a few forces acting on an airplane in flight, and Figure 5-1 captures how the required power for sustaining horizontal flight changes with speed. When plotted together with the available power, some important speeds can be determined. The difference between required and available power defines the available thrust.

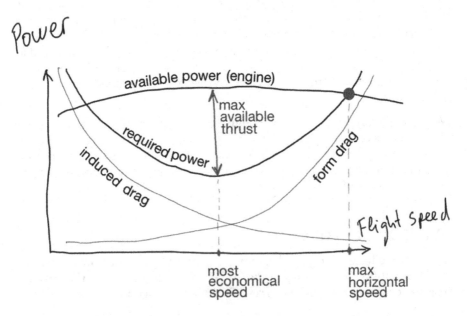

Figure 5-1. A diagram showing the available thrust of an airplane

---

[1] Jeff Sutherland and J.J. Sutherland, *Scrum: The Art of Doing Twice the Work in Half the Time* (New York: Crown Business, 2014)

At first, when trying to produce a projection, I was working with "percent allocation" of people on the project. However, allocation alone did not properly reflect the contribution people were making to software, and it also did not properly reflect the discrepancy between the actual team composition and my plans.

Since I was working as a scrum master, I knew about all the intricate issues people were having on the project. All these impediments were taking away from the time that people had available to devote specifically to writing software. Some impediments were random or temporary by nature, and some were part of the process.

For example, I found that because we were working with an offshore team where there were occasional issues with using the English language. Sometimes we had to repeat things multiple times; sometimes we had to hold an entire meeting a second time to clarify issues that were at least partly the result of the inability to use common language. I "calculated" that these diversions cost us 3% to 5% of our work time. This is about 15–20 minutes a day for the whole team, and it adds up. Another time sink was caused by a series of process-related meetings, and these meetings provided close to zero value for us as a delivery team. In the first 2 months, we attended the meetings twice a week for an hour and a half each. This alone was consuming 10% to 15% of the effective time for computer programming.

I knew that the situation would improve with time—people would start communicating more effectively, and we would be not attending the process-related meetings for much longer. Everyone was allocated 100% to the project, but I still wanted to reflect that the real contribution was less. Thus, I came up with the concept of available thrust to signify that although the team may be assigned 100% of the time on the project, the thrust people put into developing working software can be handicapped by all sorts of reasons. I couldn't use the term "utilization" as I dislike it when applied to people or teams. It implies viewing people as utilities, which I do not appreciate. Additionally, it was not representing my perception correctly, since people are still utilized when they are in a meeting, only they are not always utilized very effectively. And I also felt that "available thrust" is a more positive term and contains within itself the notion of progressive forward movement, something I kind of wanted for the project's forecast.

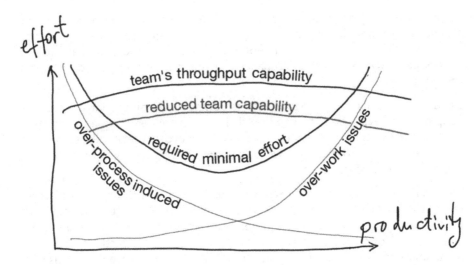

Figure 5-2. Diagram depicting the relationship between team's capability and the required effort to sustain the work on a project

Similar to the airplane's condition in flight, the actual team's throughput capability (see Figure 5-2) depends on multiple factors, and this affects a number of project conditions, such as maximum sustainable productivity and team's ability to climb out of a setback. On the left side of the diagram, the team is handicapped by bureaucracy, and on the right by being too hasty. I needed to expose this relationship between capability and required effort because I wanted to claim a certain increase in the angle of the forecast projection every time the team was able to remove any resistance factor (which would represent a higher team throughput capability curve in Figure 5-2 and a greater ability to sustain a steeper project performance). Thus, instead of just being able to say that performance will improve, I could speculate by how much it will improve. This allowed me to aim at the target with great precision. It also helped me have an adequate response when someone had overly optimistic expectations for the benefits from an expected improvement, or when someone was too negative and was diverting time into unneeded solutioning of transitory problems—often such arguments are fear driven and not based on real data. When meaningful data was available, I was able to shift discussions toward constructive outcomes more often.

For example, Figure 5-3 shows a plan where the available thrust is 70% for the first half of the project and 85% for the remainder. The actual available thrust for the first 3 months turned out to be 50% (based on factual data). The project team can determine which course of action has a real likelihood of getting the project to the desired state—whether it is freeing capacity, reducing scope, or adding new people.

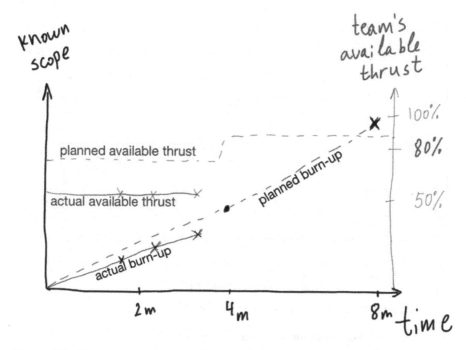

Figure 5-3. Planned and actual available thrust plotted against the project burn-up

I also wanted to reflect the fact that my team might not be at the planned staffing level. For example (see Figure 5-4), if I had planned to start with two developers, and then to have six developers working by week 8 of the project, but there were only four developers by that time, then even if they were all fully dedicated to writing software for 80% of their time, this is still only 50% of the theoretical available thrust (4 x 80% / 6 = 53%). This is important because it is surprisingly easy for people to forget what the plan is in terms of staffing commitments, yet to retain unfaltering commitments to scope and deadlines. When we fail to increase the team as planned, the project starts underperforming, yet the current delivery team can be considered to be performing as expected. With available thrust depicted, people have a clear picture from which to produce a new plan of action. By plotting everything on the timeline, clarity, with all its benefits, is restored.

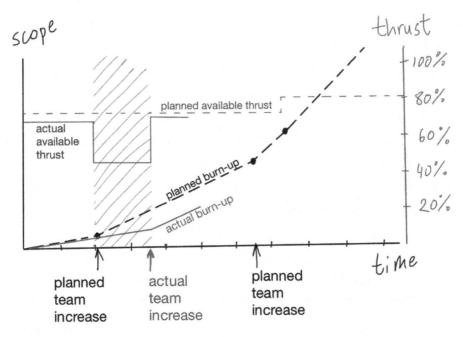

Figure 5-4. Using available thrust to control for team size increase

With available thrust we can also account for more exotic factors affecting the project, like team dissatisfaction and project politics. If we have ample information to make an argument that team members are so dissatisfied that they actually need time during the day to cope with their frustrations—more frequent walks outside, more conversations, more arguments—we can assign a percentage of time for these additional activities and subtract from the available thrust. Similarly, we can assign cost to politics and process—if team members are being pulled into meetings only to serve as a backup for arguments, or if they are pulled into unnecessary process-related meetings, a cost in terms of percentage available thrust can be assigned.

Context switching. We can "generate" available thrust, and up the angle of the projected line, by minimizing the amount of context switching. Context switching is caused by constant interruptions and fragmentation of the work in progress when working on too many things simultaneously, even if all of them contribute to the software solution. By reducing context switching, and providing an environment where programmers can zone in on their work for longer periods, we can increase the available thrust compared to an environment where these factors are not in consideration.

Measuring how much effective time we gain by minimizing context switching is not very difficult. The nonscientific way to do it is to ask a developer about how much time a day they feel is being lost from interruptions, or to add 5–15 minutes for each interruption and get an average number of interruptions.

Since context switching can easily contribute to 30–50% effective time loss (you read this correctly), it is imperative for a scrum master or project manager to familiarize themselves intimately with ways to minimize it:

- Keeping an open and functioning communication network within the team (communication does not equal chatter)

- Ensuring people are available for feedback when needed

- Guarding the team from undesired external communications (when someone, a manager maybe, comes with a random and unrelated request)

- Scheduling meetings according to how developers work[2]

- Identifying queues, applying WIP limits (work in progress limits), and facilitating short cycle times

- Having stories clearly specified[3]

- Promoting direct interaction, communication, and collaboration between all team members (improving sociometrics)[4]

These are all examples of things we can do to minimize context switching for the team. The time loss is not the only negative that comes with context switching. Sometimes brilliant ideas will disappear or never appear because the creative context was not preserved for long enough. These are losses that are difficult to measure, but not so difficult to feel.

Climbing faster. When we want to drive the angle up by adding more people to the project, we need to recognize that this is not a linear relation. Adding 30% more people does not necessarily translate in 30% gain in rate of climb.

---

[2] Paul Graham, "Maker's Schedule, Manager's Schedule," July 2009,—www.paulgraham.com/makersschedule.html
[3] Clearly specified requirement does not mean voluminous specifications. To make it more complicated, a clear specification does not guarantee shared knowledge and ease of communication. A great way to specify requirements is the subject of the book *Specification by Example* by Gojko Adzic (Shelter Island, NY: Manning Publications, 2011).
[4] Having teams where people freely communicate with each other is crucial for many aspects of high performance. Where this has a positive effect on context switching is that a novice developer will not feel the need to interrupt a chain of people and ask for assistance in initiating a discussion with another project member.

People are the single most important factor on a project, and it can affect the project both ways—adding a person might have a positive effect on the team's performance, and removing a person might also have a positive effect. We also need to account for warm-up time when adding people (see Figure 5-5). This typically shows as a short dip in the team's output followed by an increase in productivity (if the new people are contributing). The ramp-up period depends on the experience of the team members, the complexity of the domain, the relative enlargement of the team, and other factors.

Something to keep in mind is Brooks' Law, which states:

> *Adding people to a late software project makes it later.*

We need to only add people before the project is demonstrably late. By acting promptly on the available forecast indications, we can add capable team members early enough to ensure net positive effect on the project. If there are two or three planned team increases throughout the project, the cumulative "dip" from ramp-up activities can be substantial and should be accounted for during planning. It helps if scaling the team is planned and is not an afterthought.

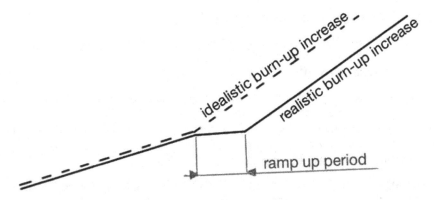

Figure 5-5. "Dip" in productivity from ramp-up activities

When applying project control by adding more people, we need to follow up with new data collection, measurements, and plotting. If the expected performance improvement is not supported by the data, we need to readjust the forecast and expectations.

Take-off and Level-off

Usually, work on a project starts slower and then accelerates a little before it stabilizes at a sustainable pace. If we simply draw a straight line from the zero point through a single data point, the performance line is more slant than needed (see Figure 5-6). If we have more than one data point, then the true project performance is captured better. For this reason, if we ever forecast on a single data point, which can be the case on a shorter project, we should adjust for this effect manually and slightly up the burn-up angle of the projection line.

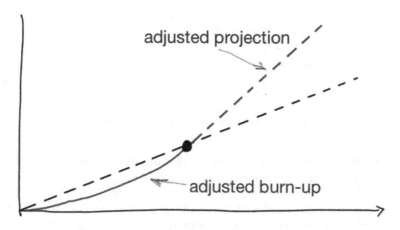

Figure 5-6. Adjusting a single data point projection for start of project activities

Somewhat similar visually, but for a different reason, is the situation at the end of a project (see Figure 5-7). Assuming a project ends with a deployment or a hand-off, then if we are aiming straight for the final date, we are effectively planning for a controlled crash on the last day of the project. Even if it is only to ensure other people's comfort, we should consider allowing for a slow-down and level-off prior to the project's final day. The project performance line should gradually go horizontal an iteration or two before the end date so that people have time to work with the software in a stabilized state. This means that we need to account for the level-off duration as it requires a slightly steeper performance slope throughout the bulk of the project. The required level-off at the end of the project effectively pushes the target scope completion sooner, thus steepening the necessary burn-up rate. This is an important consideration, especially when we are running behind schedule and figuring out the required burn-up rate that will put the project back on target.

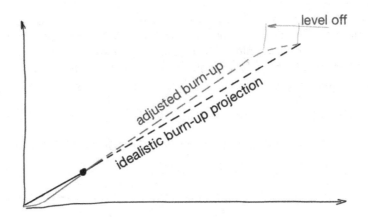

Figure 5-7. Adjusting the planned burn-up rate to allow the project to level off

The level-off adjustment might seem small, but we can't underestimate the increase in project performance that is needed to support it. The adjustment only seems small on the piece of paper on which we are plotting the graph. In reality it requires thoughtful application of the team's energy resources and a sustained effort of shielding the team from detractors throughout the project.

Health Factors

Risks and dependencies. It is common practice in software development to pull riskier items early into the project's schedule. Sometimes the opposite makes more sense—to start with the simpler things and let the team gain confidence. If the team needs to learn new technology, it might be too early for intelligent forecasting—we should work on getting people proficient first.

Provided the team is proficient, we can derisk the project by prioritizing the early iterations based on both business value and "complexity equations." Complexity equations are a set of criteria for reflecting the complexity of a piece of work and its significance for the solution's architecture. By combining the complexity factor with the business value, we can pull the technological risk early and maintain a more stable system throughout the project.

This type of adjustment is somewhat "invisible," but is not immaterial. Often people prioritize purely on business value. This is acceptable once the software development has picked up some momentum. But in the early stages, the technological factors must be reflected adequately in the priority formulation. This contributes to a healthier system and is similar to taking care of a child. When the child is very young, we think about them becoming a doctor, a mathematician, or an artist, and we read books to them to develop their brains, but we still prioritize feeding them and keeping them dry and rested first. Once they become teenagers, and hopefully by then they've developed healthy habits around eating and sleeping, we focus our energy primarily on the "business" priorities (of them becoming a doctor or an artist, etc.) and help them develop the personal qualities and capabilities that can take them there.

We need to recognize the stabilizing effect such adjustment in prioritizing strategy has on the progress of our project in its later phases. By reducing the probability for turbulence, we greatly improve the chance of the delivery team working unobstructed (by escalations and damage management activities) later in the project. We also greatly enhance the experience for clients and everyone else.

Technical health index. Every software engineer has their understanding of what represents good technical health on a software project. The effect of good technical health on the forecast is that it tightens the date range while maintaining confidence. The effect of poor health is the opposite—it flattens the normal distribution stipulated by the Central Limit Theorem and provides for less certainty in the forecast.

We can produce a technical health index by combining a set of technical indicators and evaluating the software system for each. The overall picture will represent the health index, and by maintaining it at a certain level, we can ensure satisfactory system health.

Adjusting for variability in skill set, or when working with multiple teams. If, as a scrum master or project manager, you have control over the people selection, you must select compatible people who perform comparably. You should work with the team to self-select, or ensure staffing managers are well aware of what type of people the project needs. Having a compatible team improves forecasting since it contributes to a more stable team performance. And more importantly, it improves the chances of having an awesome project. We are not going to look into interviewing techniques, but you (and the team) should consider approaching this process as a small business owner who is hiring staff for their company, and you should be as selective as you can afford.

If you are already working with a predetermined group of people, you need to facilitate equalized workload and comparable output from each of the team members, as well as collective ownership. Pair programming, frequent code reviews, and frequent demos are some of the techniques to get people to . jointly own the software solution.

If we have a reason to believe that some people or programming pairs do not perform at the level that was assumed when we were making the T-shirt size estimates, we can adjust the available thrust appropriately. For example, in a team of ten developers, where two people are consistently contributing about 50% of what everyone else is contributing, there will be 10% penalty on the overall available thrust. Remember, our job for the moment as forecasters is to collect the data. Looking for solutions, individual performance improvements being one option, is something the whole team can do together.

Scope

Dealing with new scope and scope creep. When people are faced with an increase in scope, the tensions often run high and project teams get demoralized. Developers feel that business people are trying to load them with out of scope work without comprehending the project realities, and business people feel that developers are attempting to avoid work without comprehending the need for success.

This is one more area where charts and diagrams can simplify things significantly and bring everyone closer to agreement. For this reason alone, an intelligent forecast pays for itself multiple times along the life of a single project— removing tension and allowing people to focus on meaningful problems.

When new scope starts sneaking in, we need to

- Position the new target on the forecasting diagram.
- Track new scope and original scope separately.
- Demonstrate the situation.
- Outline the available options—aim at the new target; cease the addition of new scope; extend the project; defer other scopes; or anything else that can be inferred from the forecast.

This clarity in choices dissipates tension in the team significantly. The situation is very different than adding new scope directly to a product backlog and mixing it with original scope, without a clear picture of the impact that this is having on target dates and expected features.

SCOPE DESTINATIONS

When dealing with scope, there are a few things we can do, other than completing it:

- **Deferral** of scope is when we agree to postpone implementation until all other scope is complete, that is, there is an agreement that deferred scope can be omitted from the project deliverables and still have a successful project.

- **Descoping** is when we remove scope from the project with the explicit understanding that we will no longer revisit it.

- **Reprioritization** is when we change the importance of scope with the intent to focus on the more important functionality earlier, but we still need the less important scope to be part of the project deliverables.

Additionally, if scope is organized by releases, it is useful to have fake releases labeled "*Deferred*" and "*Orphaned*". Deferred scope should be kept visible on the release level because it is still for consideration. Orphaned scope is scope that has not been assigned to a release. But just because it has not been assigned to a release does not mean there is an explicit agreement to not complete it as part of a release. It is dangerous, because sometimes orphaned scope becomes "invisible" and then all of a sudden shows up in the most inconvenient moment.

Scope, and the approach that people take to change in scope, is another junction where multiple competing concepts confuse the situation and make it easier to get in conflict. These competing concepts are product, project, and contract type.

Let's look at the common confusion between "product" and "project" first. The product-oriented view is that we can simply prioritize work by business value, in an ever-evolving backlog, and with this we guarantee that what is valued most gets completed first. However, for the people who look at the effort from the project-oriented view, it is also important to know when and at what cost will the whole effort be complete. Both views are meaningful from the perspectives of the people who maintain them. It becomes important to have a tool that can bridge the gap and help people develop an understanding and empathy for the different view.

The other pair of concepts that is easy to confuse, and affect people's attitude to scope change, is "project" and "contract." There are two main contract types in software development—one is "Fixed Price" and the other is "Time and Material." Both contract types apply some structure to the relationship of the parties. A project on the other hand, by definition, is an enterprise with a specific goal. The goal is often defined in terms of specific functionality or capabilities. The issue here is that a Fixed Price contract puts a lot of stress on software developers, while a Time and Material contract puts the stress on the client. Clients working on a project with Fixed Price contract can become insensitive to the pains of software and product developers, who are trying to stay within a set budget. And software developers working on a project with a Time and Material contract might become insensitive to the client, who is trying to accomplish a defined set of functionality before their money runs out. It is important to keep in mind that the fact that a project has a "Time and Material" contract does not invalidate the fact that the project also has a set goal (at least in the hearts and hopes of the people who initiated the project).

When we use a simple visual tool, things become clearer, with less possibility for misunderstanding. Finding satisfactory solutions becomes a controllable effort, and people are free to make clear choices from mutually complementing options. In this sense the value of a forecast goes beyond its potential accuracy. The forecast becomes a tool for communication between people who struggle finding a common language, thus saving time, projects, and relationships. This is the true power of a good forecast.

There is nothing bad with scope creep. As it happens, people discover new things they had not thought about at the start of a project or things they simply forgot to mention. This newly discovered scope often deserves to be included in the project's definition of success. As long as people are aware that it is "new," and they are still willing to keep it in their action plan, then the extra scope cannot be good or bad. It becomes simply an additional factor to consider. What is not good is when people pretend that adding new work is as simple as adding new simplistic specifications to a backlog, and that this has no implication on the rest of the project parameters like cost, duration, complexity, work environment, relationships, and more.

To facilitate the scope creep discussions, we need to keep making things more visible and easier to understand. Figure 5-8 demonstrates a situation where adding scope with the same pace will mean that only 60–70% of the originally specified functionality will be delivered by the target date. The remaining 30–40%, of what is delivered, will consist of newly identified scope. Based on this information, people can decide if they want to maintain the current "discovery rate," restrict their outreach to only what was planned, or extend the project appropriately. If needed, we can even differentiate between extra scope which reflects new knowledge and extra scope which reflects superfluous demands on an already rigorously specified system (a.k.a. gold plating).

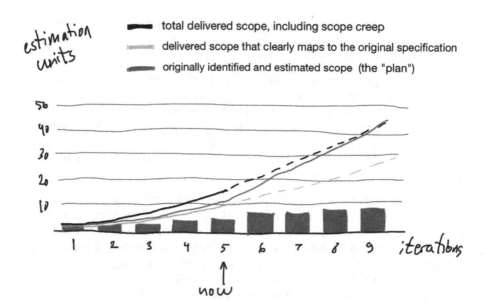

Figure 5-8. Distinguishing originally planned scope and newly added scope (scope creep)

By doing this, we can start discussing behaviors and the effects they have on the project. We can demonstrate the effect of overcomplicating previously discussed functionality, beautifying components, and gold plating. We can also demonstrate the effect of perpetual discovery, learning new things, and "pivoting."

When we provide people with ample time and a clear picture of how their actions affect the forecast, they can explore the tradeoffs and make constructive decisions, including completely reframing the project with a new set of goals and a new timeline. People can choose to maintain their behaviors in regard to scope change or they can refocus on their original plans—either way, they are aware of the situation.

Driving the Projections

Scope, duration, and cost are the dimensions which interest us most when forecasting a software development project.

- Scope is measured in effort, that is, when sizing a feature, we say, "It took 2 weeks for 3 people."

- Duration is measured in time.

- Cost is a derivative of effort and time. If you are an accountant, it is possible to measure feature size (or scope) in dollars. But in reality this dollar value can only be assigned once the effort had been expanded.

Consequently, the projections over the axes of effort and time are what we want to explore when searching for a solution in case the project is not progressing toward the desired state.

Because we employ techniques and processes that enable a sustainable pace of software development, we can extrapolate the tracking data over the remainder of the project. If we are not satisfied with the indication of the projection, we need to understand what project control to apply in order to steer the project to where we want. The balance of forces on an actual project can be rather delicate, and whatever controls we apply, we need to do it confidently, but not rushed.

We saw how available thrust and scope affect the project performance. We can use this knowledge to define a target along the effort and time dimensions and "calculate" the change in available thrust or scope required to arrive at that target. Figure 5-9 demonstrates these rough calculations: if we increase the available thrust by 30%, we have a chance of arriving at the target; alternatively, if we descope 20% of the project and only increase the available thrust with 5–10%, we also can arrive at the (new) target.

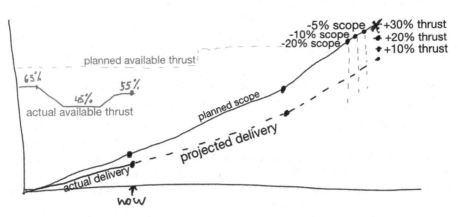

Figure 5-9. Crude calculations of required thrust increase

Let's say we decide to increase the performance angle with a quarter of its current state. We may need to do this for a number of reasons—for example, when data shows that we are tracking late with the original scope, or we are tracking well but want to move the end date sooner, or we are tracking well toward the original goal but have set eyes on a more ambitious goal. In either case this means we need "to climb" faster or for a longer period. We can consider multiple options for increasing available thrust and "calculate" how much each one contributes toward increase in project performance.

For example, if we are in a situation depicted by the preceding diagram, we might drastically cut meeting time, find process optimizations, teach new refactoring and TDD techniques, and secure 1 extra hour of work per day—this will give us 15–20% available thrust increase. We can also target less critical modules and simplify or differ functionality in order to gain the remaining bump in the projected indications. What the forecast is providing is the information we need to gain true leverage for the execution of the required improvement actions without second guessing and backtracking.

In this way we can actively drive the project performance toward a chosen state and we can apply appropriate and measured project control. Now instead of simply requesting that we have "more developers," we can say with confidence that "if we want to deliver the discussed scope for a level-off two weeks before the desired end date, then we need three more developers, who perform similarly to Jimmie and Jacqueline, to join no later than two months from now, and we need to cut status report meetings by 60% immediately."

Random and unsystematic interventions for improving the project's performance create confusion, waste time and energy, and frustrate people. By using a reliable tool for intelligent decision making and by confidently applying measured and timely control, we preserve the team's energy and keep people's relationships in the healthy area of collaboration. Not rushing when applying control allows us to do things with specific intent and anticipation. We are not in action-reaction mode anymore, but into anticipation-control mode—two very different frames of being, with material impact on the solution quality and the quality of experiences for people on the project.

Summary

Confident and fact-based forecasting is crucial for people's experiences on a project. It helps us communicate the state of the project clearly, allows us to explore the effects of various changes to project performance, and facilitates the identification of an adequate next action[5] for advancing us toward success.

---

[5] Identifying next action to move us toward a desired outcome is the step that closes the open loops as described in the stress management and productivity framework in *Getting Things Done: The Art of Stress Free Productivity* by David Allen (New York: Viking, 2001).

There are a few things that are needed in order to be successful with this method of forecasting and project control:

- An approximation of total project scope

- Proper detail of system specification

- A set of early estimations (not a forecast yet)

- Understanding of the factors affecting available thrust

- Understanding of sustainable pace—health of software system and project teams

- Tracking data of actual completion time

- Pen and paper, or a spreadsheet application like Google Sheets or MS Excel, to draw a project performance chart and forecast

Financial Performance and Managing Risks

In this chapter we will look at a tool providing additional insight into the financial health and progress of a project. We will also look at a few situations that can be expected on a typical project and how we can manage them and the associated risks.

Performance Index

The scope forecast that we explored in previous chapters enables us to apply measured project control toward desired functionality and calendar targets. Scope and time schedule are important project dimensions, but to be confident and resolute in the decision-making process, we need a clear view of the energy and financial state of the project. This will enable us to not only steer

© Dimitre Dimitrov 2020
D. Dimitrov, *Software Project Estimation*,
https://doi.org/10.1007/978-1-4842-5025-9_7

the controls to where we want but also to have an informed expectation for the longer-term capability of the project.

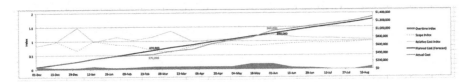

Figure 6-1. A chart depicting five project performance metrics that highlight the financial aspect of a project

The indication of available thrust already provides deep insight into the project's condition. However, available thrust is more about the team's output than about the project's. The team might be hitting all the planned functionality targets, but at a higher than planned dollar cost, and thus the scope forecast alone is not sufficient. We can plot the planned[1] and actual dollar expenses, along with a few index values that provide information for the financial health of the project. Figure 6-1 shows a combination of five project performance metrics overlaid on the same diagram. We explore them in detail through the remainder of the chapter. I call this combined representation of the project's performance—the performance index.

Similar to the spreadsheet files from Chapter 4, there are sample spreadsheet files with data and charts demonstrating how to build a performance index. For those readers who enjoy spreadsheet formulas and charts, the sample spreadsheets and diagrams in Appendix B at the end of the book—and can be downloaded from www.apress.com/9781484250242 —might facilitate your familiarization with the details of the method further.

A set of simple indications which improve awareness of the project's financial and energy state are

- Money burn—planned cost and actual cost
- Value index—scope ("value") we have delivered to date compared to planned

---

[1] For projects with a fixed scope and fixed budget contract, the planned cost is clear. For projects with time and material contracts, there is no agreed-upon cost, but that does not prevent us from planning or establishing a desired cost, or at least indicating the projected cost.

- Relative cost index—money we have spent per unit of scope compared to planned
- Borrowing index—the overtime we have borrowed from employees in order to be where we are

The performance indexes diagram shows the project from a different perspective, and we gain new sensitivity to changing circumstances compared to only tracking on scope. By having two qualitatively distinct perspectives, we get to "triangulate" our position and to steer the project with much more adequacy and confidence.

Burning more money than planned is not always something negative. If we are producing proportionally more value than planned, then this is in fact an unexceptional situation. In this case the money burn will indicate a departure of the actual cost from the planned cost, but the value index and relative cost index will remain close to each other. Both planned cost and actual cost graphs are shown in dollars and plotted against the secondary vertical axis on the diagram in Figure 6-1. The value index and relative cost index are unitless values, and their graphs are plotted against the main vertical axes on the diagram in Figure 6-1.

If the value index and relative cost index diverge, we know we are burning money faster than we are producing value. We then need to start looking for ways to reduce the money burn or to increase the productivity. If reality and expectations are irreconcilable, reframing and renegotiation of the project is in order.

This analytical tool gives us an opportunity to identify problems and start working on them earlier. By pulling the moment of awareness sooner, and by bringing additional clarity to important project facets, we are given a larger span of time for an effective action before the latest responsible moment.

If you look at the spreadsheet formulas, you will notice that the inverse of the money burn is factored into the value index to amplify its indication. An amplified indicator alerts us more promptly when things go astray. For example, let's say we have a plan to add two developers to a team of eight, and expect to ultimately achieve a 17% increase in the team's performance (17% is approximately 1/6th). Let's say the actual increase in scope completion (after 3 weeks of ramp-up) is about 10%. If we only track for scope and we look at how the slope of the scope forecast is steepening, it might take us some time before we realize that the increase in team's performance is not enough compared to planned. With an amplified indication, when comparing the value index to the relative cost index, we get alerted of things not going as desired almost immediately.

This can be seen on Figure 6-2 where the graphs on the top reflect the scope track, and the graphs on the bottom show the corresponding behavior on the value index and the relative cost index. Index deviation is not the same as actual scope deviation from desired scope. If the planned burn-up is not steep, then even if the two indexes diverge significantly, the lag in terms of "scope not delivered" will be small (the scenario on the left side of Figure 6-2). And the opposite—if the planned burn-up is steeper, then a divergence in the performance indexes is accompanied with a larger scope deviation (the scenario on the right side of Figure 6-2).

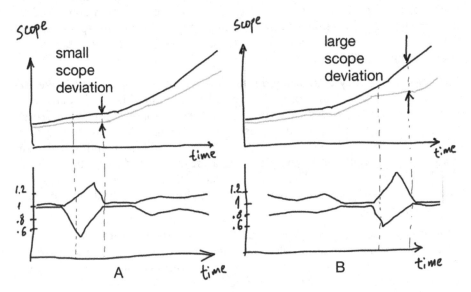

Figure 6-2. The performance indexes at the bottom and the correlated behavior of the project in terms of scope delivery at the top

This amplified indication should be used for prompt initiation of situation analysis and not for triggering a knee jerk reaction or panic. It is important to understand that the departure of these indexes from one another only signifies some change in the trends. The effect on the project's progress might be less dramatic. Even when we observe the indexes departing sharply, we still need to analyze the situation first and apply measured and careful control only after gaining sufficient understanding of the indications. If we have a small team and we are planning to gradually increase it, then if we observe the indexes departing sharply, indicating that we are producing much less than planned, we may conclude that this will be compensated quickly later, when additional developers come on board. The early team might be laying the groundwork with fundamental software architecture, which we know will pay for itself later when the new developers can reap the benefits of working on a healthy system. The situation might not be matching the plan, yet it might not necessitate an immediate intervention either. Because early or mid-project performance is not a success determining factor in and of itself, we can allow ourselves some time before springing into action. On the other hand, if our analysis indicates things are deteriorating for the long run, we can get on it quickly and have more time to generate viable options.

Borrowing Index

Overtime is shown on the diagram in Figure 6-1 as a percentage of the normal work time and measured on the primary vertical axis with 1 being 100% (or 8 hours of overtime per day). When it comes to borrowing, different companies do things differently. Some borrow recklessly, some never borrow, and some are in between. Some return what they borrowed and some don't. Companies that are (very) mature in their adoption of the agile software development principles reject the idea of overtime vehemently. However, not all companies and managers are at such a level of agile maturity. Some do not understand the essence of sustainable work or the 40-hour workweek principle and regularly request overtime. When managers do this, they need to acknowledge the fact that a portion of the output is being covered with effort for which they have not planned (and frequently are not paying for it[2]).

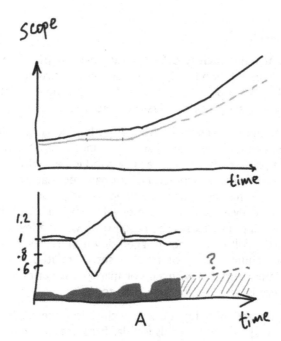

Figure 6-3. Delivering according to a plan with the help of "hidden" overtime contributions

---

[2] As a scrum master or project manager, it is our responsibility to talk to managers and find out whether overtime is being paid and at what rate, or whether people get compensated in other ways like extra vacation or training.

Figure 6-3 shows a possible scenario where we are happily forecasting green project status based on the actual delivery data (the actual delivery very slightly lagging than planned as indicated by the graph at the top of the figure). But can the rate of overtime, as indicated by the shaded area on the bottom chart, be sustained through the remaining half of the project? And even if it can be sustained—is this the right way to plan and manage a project?

It might be uncomfortable for many project managers to bring overtime to the surface, but tracking how much time is borrowed and keeping management informed is an important energy management activity. Overtime saps the energy of the team and affects the dynamics on the project. The nature of this "loan," like any other loan, is cumulative, and this is why it's plotted as an area chart so that the magnitude of time borrowed to date can be appreciated. The information from the overtime graph does not help us get immediate performance improvements, but it helps us navigate the treacherous waters of overtime and exposes a major contributor to a deteriorating environment. If we observe that the project is staying "on track" by continually borrowing time from employees, then we should look for other solutions!

Working Smart

Keep the initial estimation effort tiny and simple. If we spend too much time for the estimation itself, then it becomes a project on its own, and no one needs this. A big portion of the estimation time is usually spent with the initial breaking of scope to the desired resolution.

Sometimes clients come prepared with a large functional specification document. These documents have a lot of shortcomings when it comes to actually building the right product, but they are very good for establishing the baseline of what is expected from the project. Functional specifications can be decomposed fairly easy to the resolution we need. A single person (e.g., a scrum master, a business analyst, or a software developer) can break this down into enough pieces to support the desired resolution within a few hours of work. It takes just a little skill to not get bogged down in irrelevant details and to keep carving out chunks that comprise a set of related functionality. The chunks can be simply outlined with a color marker on a printed version of the specification; there is no need for high-tech toolset.

Or sometimes, instead of a functional specification, we might work with a story map. Story maps are great tools for clarifying product vision. We need to make sure the map has enough stories to support the desired resolution from forecasting perspective. For a decently sized project, this should not be an issue. However, if we end up with too few stories, then we need to probe the product owner or business analyst for additional detail. Chances are that if there are too few items in the story map, then they need to be broken down further within the iterations, and probing for more detail is not a wasted effort.

Occasionally, a product owner has already broken down everything into a big flat backlog, and he/she is ready to take us through the requirements that are captured in it. If this happens, we need to be very careful to not confuse the estimates for the forecasting with the estimates for the story points. It is likely there will be a strong correlation between both, but we need to protect the team from artificial pressure of low-level estimation at this point, and we should keep story point estimation for later when we have iteration planning meetings and the team has more detail and current context.

Keeping things simple, and even intentionally sketchy, is important when it comes to estimation and forecasting. The first reason is that we simply don't want to do too much work and spend too much money on it. Estimation and forecasting are activities that many people perceive as overhead already, and asking for a sizable effort toward them will be met with resistance. The second reason, which is probably the main one, is that we don't want to get too attached to the estimation results.

Keep the starting data around. Long-term estimates do not become useless when we gain new knowledge and update the scope of the solution. We can incrementally adjust only the things that did change, and we can analyze the effect this has on the projected performance. Are we going to need more available thrust? Do we need to cut scope elsewhere or lengthen the project?

If there is a decision to change the scope of the solution, we need to update the targets and baseline, but it is best to keep the historical data as well. This way we can backtrack and reevaluate when "calculations" seem off. The effort that goes into rebasing is usually not that large. If we notice that we need to rebase the project all the time and that any long-term planning gets invalidated within an iteration or two, then we need to figure out what are the issues around product direction and vision. Those issues will not be solved by pumping out software.

Short-term estimates are not useless either. Short projects are always harder to forecast. On projects shorter than 3 months, and with less than three to four developers, it becomes difficult to get to the required resolution and to produce a meaningful projection early enough for decision-making insights. For this reason, a forecast on such projects is less useful as a project control tool and is more useful as a communication tool.

The best control tool on short projects will always be relentless prioritization, deferral, and descoping because there is just no time to improve team performance by adding people or adopting better development practices. This is not to say that on long projects we should take prioritization casually—we need to always ensure we are working on important things and we are not implementing features with low utility. A forecasting diagram on a short project can serve as a great tool for communicating the importance of prioritization and deferral to clients by demonstrating an unattainable target sooner.

We have to be cautious when adding people on short projects. We should consider this option only if we are certain that the new team members can start contributing immediately, and that the new team remains compatible. In practice, this means that everyone is very proficient, and the problems we are solving with the software are not challenging. If introducing new team members will destabilize the project, we should explore other ways to increase available thrust—improving requirements so developers spend less time in useless discussions, removing unnecessary process-related meetings, normalizing acceptance criteria across features so there is less repetition, and so on. Cutting meetings is good to a point, but shaving off interaction time excessively can achieve the opposite effect on team's performance.

Short projects can be riskier for another subtle reason—it is more likely that business people went into such projects with less thinking and preparation than what they would expend for a longer project. There is an increased chance that the business team wants to add new features they forgot to consider at the beginning. Often these change requests are legitimate and scope needs to be added. By tracking and demonstrating both the projections for the originally discussed scope and the newly added scope, we can help people make intelligent choices.

Honesty. Because we want to invest as little time as possible in collecting data and producing charts, there will be instances where it's just easier to round up a number or move things around. For example, functionality might have been finished a few days after the iteration is over, but we know that most of the work was performed within it, so we count the scope toward the totals for that iteration. Or sometimes we know something is incomplete, but we consider it finished anyway because developers told us they'll be merging code in 2 hours. As long as we do these things infrequently, and with a clear conscience, then we can trust the forecast just the same as if we were able to plug in the exact true data.

We should keep a record of any manipulations and doctoring of data we had to perform. And we should be ready to outline the essence of our activities to the business decision makers if they probe deeper into our analysis. If managers or clients need the data itself, and not only charts, we have to supply the actual details. We should only discuss data details in terms of their impact on the confidence in the forecast and avoid qualifying data details as good or bad.

Making the right calls in difficult situations. Sometimes we have a forecast that shows we are tracking short, but clients will say the scope is non-negotiable, they want it all. Don't get alarmed. Or at least not right away.

First, look for the usual suspects for lifting the curve up—fewer meetings, quicker feedback from people with business insight, more and capable people on the team, simplified implementation (without impacting functionality). Deferred scope has been stated by the client as "out of the question," but we shouldn't stop asking questions—we need an explicit statement of value for every suspicious system element. We need to look for innovative solutions and for scope that we can safely get rid of. If clients don't agree on deferring, maybe they can agree on simplifying it.

Work on reprioritizing and deferring scope needs to happen with as little participation from developers as possible. While the project manager and business people are working on deferring scope, developers should be working on the highest priority features that have already been validated. We should only involve developers if this will enrich their context in a useful way.

Once we have carefully examined what can be done, we can calculate the contribution these changes might have to available thrust or scope, and we can present new options to clients.

When looking for "extra time," be careful to not completely wipe out the level-off needed toward the end of the project. This will translate into a very rough end of the project and will leave people with an unpleasant experience. It will also remove safety for your team.

In case the forecast indicates timely coverage of all the desired scope, we should still prioritize, simplify, and descope. Occasionally there are small things that clients have not considered as separate pieces of scope, but once it is pointed out, they might be willing to drop them. There are few things that give more positive feedback to a technical team than a project manager or scrum master who cares to make their lives better by identifying work that can be removed. And a happy delivery team can work wonders.

Projects like this, where clients want it all, are probably the typical projects. We need to find a way to sustain the delivery efforts throughout the project. Just because we made the right call once does not mean we don't have to work hard for the rest of the project. Opportunities for descoping should be sought daily and hourly.

Not making the wrong calls in easy situations. When things are going well, we should stay vigilant and keep looking for opportunities to simplify scope and improve environment. Everything that gets worked on should have clear purpose and value. If we splurge by working on questionably valuable features when things are going well, it can be difficult to reeducate people quickly enough when we need to apply discipline to every decision.

Sometimes it is easier to make a decision after you compare how things work in practice. So people might be inclined to initiate an A/B test. But making production software with the purpose of experimenting is not cheap. Just because companies like Google are setting up A/B testing for various usability aspects of their applications does not mean it is a good idea to apply the same approach on any project. Such experiments can be expensive in terms of software architecture and maintenance, and there might be cheaper, albeit less certain, methods of gaining valuable knowledge.

When things are going well, extra scope might even come from developers. They can get so excited that they start building things they find useful. This is tricky. We should not overdo project control and kill people's enthusiasm and inventiveness, but we do need to keep reminding everyone to stay on course. Doing things for the client at no additional cost is very nice, but it might not be nice enough to offset their negative experience should a desired feature get inadvertently dropped later in the project. Prioritization and scope control should be exercised judiciously regardless of how the project is tracking.

When other people make "wrong" calls, save the relationships and not the forecast. When working to get a difficult project to success, it is all too easy to consider events that derail our plans as wrong. If everyone else on the project is okay with adding scope and affecting the forecast, the scrum master or project manager can simply change the forecast. Resisting a change in the project only because the schedule and forecast need an update is never a valid position and is a definite sign of not understanding the needs of the people on the project. (If the updated forecast indicates we need to reframe the project, then this is another problem for people to work on. Reframing a project is not an indication of failure.)

Navigating Issues

When business people do not want to engage with prioritization. Sometimes people do not know how to prioritize, or they don't want to. They just cannot get into action mode. Our job, as project managers and scrum masters, is to help them make the right choices. It is not to make the choices for them. We should understand what is blocking them from deciding and treat this as any other blocker on the project—that is, it is our responsibility to have the blocker removed.

It is okay if people do not make decisions right away. We only need them to acknowledge awareness of an explicit "latest responsible time" for a decision. Being aware of the latest responsible moment is a powerful motivator.

When people insist on waterfall type of project management and reports. Sometimes, we haven't had time to collect data yet, but we are being asked to have a forecast anyway. It might even come as a request for a Gantt chart. Producing a forecast takes a day or a few, and ruining relationships over it might cost the project. My choice usually is to produce one and to supply whatever explanations are needed to ensure the consumers of the forecast have adequate understanding of the reality.

In this case, we should add extra adjustments (such as in the examples that follow) and provide an optimistic, pessimistic, and "likely" date. Do not provide a single date even if people choose to only focus on one of the dates you provide in the range.

We should add buffers to the timeline for anything that represents risk. One team-hour is equal to 2.5–3% of the workweek budget, and the percentages can accumulate quickly. We are mostly concerned with the effort of the developers—programmers, designers, and testers. If a scrum master is in status report meetings for 50% of the day, this doesn't necessarily affect the available thrust negatively, it might even be a good thing.

Here are example safety buffers that I have applied to projects when converting from "estimated effort" to "calendar time":

- 5–10% of the calendar time is for holidays and vacations.

- 5% of calendar time is for sick and personal time.

- 2–5% of the effort (and money) can go for ramp-up activities.

- 2–5% of the effort (and money) can go for level-off activities.

- 10–15% of the calendar time is for the basic project-related meetings.

- 2–10% of the effort and money can go toward additional team communication. Every time the team increases with four to five people, this percentage needs adjustment. It is more expensive to have larger teams.

- 2–10% of the effort can go for additional conference calls and emails with other locations, regardless of whether it is a remote client or a dispersed delivery team. It is more expensive to have teams that are not colocated.

- Working on a legacy system?—Add 25–50% to your estimated effort right off the bat, and be prepared to adjust even more as you start collecting data.

- Account for any nondelivery work that applies to delivery team and assign cost in terms of % team time. If the work only applies to one team member, then prorate the load appropriately:

  - Regulatory process.

  - Alien project management process and procedures—if the team is being asked to follow an alien process. Often this is the case when working for a client on their site and in tight collaboration with their teams.

- Technical documentation/user manuals—if the team needs to write more than what they naturally perceive as sufficient level of software documentation.

- Travel/business trips—If someone is going to another office, they will work on code less.

- Delivery team training—if the delivery team needs training or needs to provide training.

- Time sheets—Sometimes a scrum master (SM) can help people on the team with this, sometimes not (depending on the setup, this can easily account for 1–2% of the time in the week for every individual on the team).

- Security procedures and dealing with foreign systems (logging in, switching networks, VPN, etc.) for Dev and for QA—Sometimes people are forced to work in less than optimal development environments for security reasons, and it's not unheard of to have spent 10–15 min logging into an ancient system; this should be reflected as % cost to the project.

Figure 6-4 shows the percentage available thrust that we can reclaim by contributing time for actual software development back to the working day. The percentages are based on 5 hours of work toward working software per day, which is probably on the high end for a typical developer.

Activity duration	The whole team			Single developer
	Once per week	Twice per week	Every day	
5 min	0.33%	0.66%	1.5%	divided by # of developers
10 min	0.5%	1%	3%	
15 min	1%	2%	5%	
30 min	2%	4%	10%	
1 hour	4%	8%	20%	

Figure 6-4. Percentage available thrust per unit of working time

It is worth guarding against many of these in the Assumptions or Risks sections of a SOW (Statement of Work). We can introduce clauses in the form of

> "Assumptions: No more than 1 hour per week required for managing client networks and systems."

I know that the Manifesto for Agile Software Development puts relationships over contracts, but SOW will be around for a long time as a tool, and there is nothing wrong with coming up with a good and meaningful SOW document if we are signing one anyway. This is especially relevant for Fixed Price contracts, but it won't hurt even in a Time and Material contract so that we draw attention to activities and risks that can be costly for the project.

Deadlines produced by a senior manager or a VIP client, without input from developers on the project, are an immediate red flag that needs to be reflected in the project status report, and it should remain red until there is data to support the deadline. Sometimes people in senior roles manufacture a date on their own and say, "we need to just start working and be done by November 20th." This is okay as a method of getting things going, but we need to make it immediately visible that, as far as a desired project end date is concerned, there is nothing to support the "plan." By immediately calling out an unsupported deadline (by "coloring" the status red), we ensure that people are working with the correct understanding of the project's reality.

When clients or managers confuse velocity and forecasting. Sometimes clients grow impatient and, because they see the team assigning story points each iteration, they will ask the team to assign points to all the stories until the end of the project. And they expect that the team subsequently commits to covering X number of points per sprint[3] from now until the last sprint.

This is an indication that people are experiencing difficulties in transitioning from project paradigm to a product paradigm. We need to work with them to clarify the distinctions and adjust expectations.

As clients get some exposure to agile development practices, they might confuse story points with project estimation. We need to not get confused though. Story points help with keeping consistent pace when going from one sprint to another. We only need story points to prevent the team from inadvertently taking in too much work within a sprint.

When clients want the whole project estimated in points. Same thing as earlier, only it happens at the start of the project. They might have heard

---

[3] Sprint is the name for an iteration in one of the more popular frameworks for running agile development projects—Scrum. Scrum claims to be project and product framework, but in reality it is more of a product framework (www.scrumalliance.org).

about story points, and they think they are for project estimation. We need to make sure they can start differentiating between story points and project estimation, and then we can proceed with the forecasting method as explained in this book.

Estimating bugs. We need to consider bugs as "cost of our practices," or as "resistance," and subtract some amount from the available thrust. For example, we can subtract 20% from the available thrust and apply this over the remainder of the project. If we want to be even more correct, we should find an exponential function to reflect this technical debt cost, since a cost for fixing a bug increases the longer the bug stays in existence within a growing system. For example, we can subtract an additional 2% with every subsequent iteration.

If there is a rolling wave of bugs, we may need to subtract as much as 80%. This, of course, is an extremely unhealthy situation, and forecasting is likely not the first priority on a project like this. But it is exactly in moments like this when senior managers want even more reports and projections. If we do have to forecast, a 20% available thrust means that if something is estimated as 1 day of effort, it now takes 5 days of effort, and with the slew of meetings and context interruptions on a dysfunctional projects like this, it can mean 10 or more days on the calendar.

When people ask for precise release forecast. If we are committing to a fixed scope release every 2–3 months, we are in effect doing small waterfall projects. It is difficult to forecast with good precision on a 2–3-month timeline.

However, many times releases are only "internal" and software does not get deployed in production on every "release." In this case we have to learn why it is important to get to this level of precision. If it turns out it is not that important, we can negotiate to forecast only for the full project and to only provide a brief outlook for the internal releases. Remember, sometimes clients, managers, or business people will come up with an ask simply out of a habit or because they are not aware of the actual cost associated with it. Again, scrum masters and project managers can treat instances of this as impediments to the project and treat them accordingly, that is, by figuring out better solutions.

When things don't pan out right. Sometimes we are 2–3 months into a long project and we observe we are well behind the desired state. Clients and other VIPs will often insist on "improved" estimation and forecasting. We might be asked to go over all the scope again and redo the estimation with the mandate to produce a more precise number.

If this happens, and if there is a valid reason to doubt the forecast's quality, do not go for better precision or accuracy of individual estimates, go for better resolution. It is easy to just push the pressure onto the delivery team and ask them for more precise estimates, or ask BAs for more detailed specification and then ask developers for improved precision of estimations. This is detrimental to the team and will not produce any form of improvement. The power of initial estimates is not in their accuracy, but in their numbers. A large number of estimates, each with low accuracy, makes for a forecast that is significantly more likely to be accurate than a forecast based on few detailed and "precise" estimates. Detailed requirements do not facilitate precision of estimation. However, they facilitate breaking down work in a greater number of chunks. This in turn improves the forecast quality.

When clients or managers ask for overtime. We need to find out what are the expected achievements from such an ask. Is the extra 1% of functionality coverage, that we get out of a stolen Saturday, worth inconveniencing the people on the team and creating an unhealthy working environment? Is the extra 1% we get for that single day of overtime going to be followed by a whole week of subpar productivity from everyone on the team? What will be the net % contribution toward the project? Do we need to extend the landing (and the project) with another week instead?

When we ask these questions, we should do it against the forecast diagram. We need to improve the visibility of what we are gaining and what we are losing, so that the decisions are informed and the discussions don't deteriorate into dysfunctional arguments.

Chasing quality through documentation. There will be clients with a rigid project management process and clumsy procedures. When we are asked to comply with extraneous processes, escalation procedures, and endless paper trail, we need to subtract that time, which affects the delivery team, from the available thrust. It is sometimes scary to do, when you realize that people are only left with 20% of their day to actually work toward a software solution. But if the information is presented considerately, it can educate people outside the delivery team on where to improve impeding processes. We also need not share the actual forecast and all its details. If the environment is not conducive to limitless transparency, we might be better off keeping the forecast and data to ourselves, while negotiating the terms of the project with a newly gained perspective and confidence.

When people argue on scope. You'll sometimes hear people start arguing about whether something is in scope or out of scope. Working with imprecise terms like "too much" and "scope" brings confusion. Additionally, some people think "out of scope for the project," and some people think "in scope for the product."

When we can clearly show which pieces of the product are making it in the current project envelope, the discussions become much more focused and misunderstandings much more unlikely. For this reason we need to keep asking for prioritized product backlog and then draw the line where the project envelope intersects with the (product) backlog.

When people insist on fixed everything—scope, time, money, and quality. We need to remind people that we, all of us who are working on the project, can only manage the project within the envelope of what is real. A forecast is not a tool for improving the project's performance nor is it a tool for project control. It is only a tool for visualizing the performance and facilitating the control. Just because someone wishes two lines to intersect somewhere else on a diagram does not mean the project is under control. People need to follow up with specific and intentional actions.

Remember—project and product are two different things. People might be trying to squeeze the whole product within a single project. We should revisit the project goals and examine each of the proposed product capabilities against the goals. If some product features seem less vital, they become good candidates for deferral and descoping.

The true controls for project performance are

- Managing scope, including simplifying the requirements
- Improving people's understanding of the requirements
- Managing throughput/available thrust
- Improving people's environment

If the business people are not willing to engage with any of these controls, and the only suggested control is "just get it done," we need to explain that the project is not being controlled toward any different outcome than what it is rolling toward on its own.

If the forecast is showing that the project is behind schedule, but people want to just wait and see if it is going to steer toward the better outcome on its own, then this is a valid decision. If the forecast makes us 80% certain in our claims that a project will be late, then there is a 20% chance we are not right. Business people are free to take this chance.

What to do when projections don't materialize? We need to maintain a constant watch on the situation once projections have been communicated. We need to speak up early. Usually we are the first to know when the projections start going south. Also, as project managers and scrum masters, we need to not get in a rut and become mere bookkeepers or statisticians—we need to actively help other people and drive the project toward its objectives with every opportunity we have.

Navigating Issues with the Team

When team members ask what is the point of estimating when it is not accurate? We might get this question from developers or managers on our team. People might resist providing estimates, or foot the bill for time spent on estimation, when they honestly believe we cannot provide what they consider to be of value—namely, accuracy and precisions. We need to explain the power of statistics and how it translates to precision.

What a project manager or scrum master can do is to explain the approach in this book quickly and make it known that no one is being asked to provide precise individual estimates. The estimation ranges overlap to highlight this lack of precision, and we need this only as one of the inputs into a forecast. The forecast itself is generated later and only after the team starts producing real software, and we can map real data to the initial guesswork.

If people on the team do not trust the approach, we can still ask them to donate a few hours of their time to help with this as an experiment. We should prepare for the estimation session well, so we don't waste any of their time on activities we could have completed ourselves. We might not get too many chances at this.

Why do we need to estimate in the beginning when we are giving story points later anyway? This is the same issue as the one described in "When clients or managers confuse velocity and forecasting." We need to explain that story points are not ideal for project forecasting.

How is this different than the "mythical man-month"? Remember Brooks' Law: "Adding manpower to a late software project makes it later."

The method in this book is different because we are not establishing a one-to-one relationship between a man-month and the output of a team. We are identifying a functional relationship between effort, time, and output. We account for the changes in this relationship when different parameters of the project change—team size, time in meetings that don't contribute to software, issues with environment, communication difficulties, and many more. We are also not treating all people equally. We can adjust the functional relationship to account for most of the factors we are aware of.

And finally, one of the main benefits of a reliable forecast is that we can prove we need to add people to the project before the project is "late." When the realization of a project being late happens in the last quarter of a project, there is no time to save it by adding more people. When this realization happens in the first quarter or earlier, then adding people is not necessarily inadequate.

Summary

Tracking the deliverables of a project and making intelligent scheduling projections is a critically important task in project management. However, having knowledge for scope alone is not sufficient for reliably navigating toward success. Gaining understanding for the financial performance of a project provides valuable and rich context for project management decisions and can highlight issues much sooner. We learn the answers to questions like

- Are we spending more money than planned for the delivered functionality?

- Is our project staying afloat thanks to the "volunteering" work of the delivery team?

- Do we have enough money to take us to the end of the project?

In order to gather the information for producing intelligent scope forecasts and financial performance index indicators, we need to set up appropriate expectations, to manage appropriate conditions, and to navigate certain situations that arise on most software development projects. If we approach environmental risks without proper consideration, we might introduce instability on the project that cannot be captured by a forecasting model. Managing risks wisely, and maintaining an environment where everyone feels safe, is an important aspect of ensuring that intelligent forecasting and project management is a viable option.

Tidbits

A tasty soup of loosely related concepts, heuristics, and practical details is mixed up in this appendix with the intent to provide the important nutrients for anyone who applies intelligent forecasting in practice. There will be situations that require coming up with innovative applications of the methods described in this book. Having the required nutrition will aid in developing the intuition and skill for practical application.

Software Development Laws

Throughout this book I've referred to Brooks' Law and Gall's Law. I've gathered them, and others, here and expanded on how they related to project estimation and forecasting.[1] I've also added few other important software development principles for quick reference, as they capture important properties of the reality on software development projects.

Brooks' Law

Brooks' Law: "Adding manpower to a late software project makes it later."

Brooks' Law is sometimes generalized as

Adding people to software development slows it down.

---

[1] Some of the ideas in this section have been exercised in Allan Kelly's book, *Xanpan* (Leanpub, 2018), and I've reexpressed them along with my additions as it relates to the concepts in the main body of this book.

© Dimitre Dimitrov 2020
D. Dimitrov, *Software Project Estimation*,
https://doi.org/10.1007/978-1-4842-5025-9

It is important to note here that the generalized form is just that, a generalization. It is true, but only for a set period that follows immediately after adding people to the project. Once the new team members have had time to ramp up and start contributing, the net throughput of development might increase (depending on many other factors).

The original version of this principle is important for project control because it tells us that people should be added to a project only in anticipatory mode, that is, planned. If we are reactively adding people because we have realized that the project is late, then it is too late.

As said earlier in the book, forecasting can help with this situation since it puts us exactly in the anticipatory mode needed for sensible project control. We can decide whether more people are needed in advance of "being late."

Gall's Law

> Gall's Law: "A complex system that works is invariably found to have evolved from a simple system that worked. A complex system designed from scratch never works and cannot be patched up to make it work. You have to start over with a working simple system."

Gall's Law is about growing software systems. It explains how complex but working systems become in existence.

This principle can be applied to software teams as well and has important implications on scaling teams or working on projects with large teams (five small scrum teams working on the same project comprise a larger project team).

> A complex team that works is invariably found to have evolved from a simple team that worked. A complex team designed from scratch never works and cannot be patched up to make it work. You have to start over with a working simple team.

This law basically says that we need to grow teams, and not scale them or "architect" them. This is important, since growing a team does not have to start with adding more people. We can first exhaust the practical opportunities for growth and improvement within the small and simple team, including teaching them new skills. One of the benefits of this is that when we have a team of high performing individuals, adding new individuals causes much less disturbance. The new people tend to accelerate quicker because most of their interactions are having the right support and this builds their confidence. This feeds into an organically sustainable growing mechanism—as long as we don't exceed the intake capacity of the highly proficient team.

Many frameworks for applying structure at scale attempt to slice and dice a large project team into small groups and hope to achieve the efficiency of the small group, but simply applied at scale. My experience with this approach is not positive. Large teams that are broken in multiple small teams are still large teams. They need to be grown. Once we start with a normal sized team and grow it beyond its natural capacity, we can add more people and then split it in two. Then keep growing each of the teams gradually until we are able to split in two again. Of course, we need to account for a great many number of other factors if we are to build a high performing team. But starting with a large team, or many small teams, is a sure way to create significant drag from the get-go.

Starting a project with a large team puts the project in a state of being late as soon as it has started (because the team cannot be patched to function). Projects like this operate under Brooks' Law at all times, and we are stuck in a death spiral where the more people we add, the less chance we have for making it out unscathed.

Parkinson's Law and Hofstadter's Law

Parkinson's Law: "Work expands so as to fill the time available for its completion."

Hofstadter's Law: "It always takes longer than you expect, even when you take into account Hofstadter's Law."

These two principles are true when we look at a project as a single monstrous task and we grand-total the small tasks into a single large effort. With the method of intelligent forecasting, we in fact treat each chunk of work as a small project with its own probability of being on time, early, or late. We then utilize the Central Limit Theorem to work on all the probabilities together, accounting for the effect of each one, while not focusing on any one individually. We are also tracking the project performance with additional project indexes, which provide a fine-grained survey and prevent the work from simply expanding and compressing within the full project envelope.

Conway's Law

Conway's Law: "Organizations which design systems ... are constrained to produce designs which are copies of the communication structures of these organizations."

Conway's Law can be applied to multiple aspects of software teams and the systems they build. In the context of forecasting, it reinforces Gall's Law because if we want to start with a small and simple system, we also need a small team working on it. Otherwise, if we start with a complex team, even if the system starts small, it will inherit the complexities of the large team through an overly complex design and architecture. A complex team will not be able to produce a simple solution. This will immediately affect the team's ability to work in a sustainable way, and the result is often legacy systems even before they have been deployed to production.

Manifesto for Agile Software Development

The Manifesto for Agile Software Development[2] is a document that gives valuable perspectives on a few core dimensions of life on a software project. The manifesto is a document that is worth reflecting on, and people working with scrum or other frameworks related to agile development should take time to discuss what applies to their projects and where they want to seek improvements. Because there are some very popular misinterpretations of what is in the manifesto, especially as it relates to project management and planning, I feel it is important to go for a quick dive. First, take a look at Figure A-1 to read the original manifesto in its entirety.

---

[2]http://agilemanifesto.org

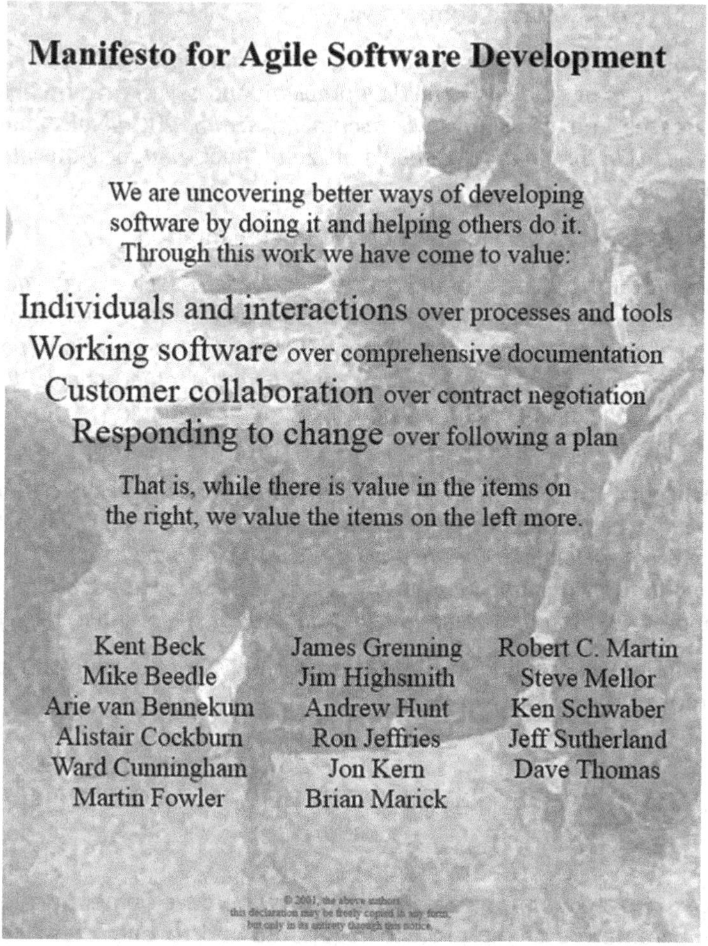

Figure A-1. The manifesto as shown at http://agilemanifesto.org

What follows is a line-by-line examination of the manifesto with my thoughts on how it is relevant to forecasting projects. My commentary is in italic.

Manifesto for Agile Software Development

We are uncovering better ways of developing software (*A "hint" that this is primarily about software development and not about project delivery. Better software development enables better project delivery but does not replace it or guarantee it.*) by doing it and helping others do it.

Through this work we have come to value:

Individuals *(clients, managers, developers, and scrum masters are individuals. We need to treat them as such and value their problems and issues)* **and interactions** over processes and tools *(agile development, scrum, XP, #NoEstimates, and estimates all fall in this group. We should utilize the tools that facilitate interactions with individuals.)*

Working software over comprehensive documentation

Customer collaboration *(working together implies taking care of each other's needs. It cannot be one sided where developers only care for better software and business people only care for business)* over contract negotiation *(positioning yourself well for a possible negotiation, and enabling other people to reason productively during negotiation, is good. Contract negotiation is different than project negotiation.)*

Responding to change *(knowing what the change means, in the context of the project, is important for an adequate response. Baselining, tracking, forecasting, and planning are not useless activities as they put change in context.)* over following a plan *(trying to follow a static plan at any cost is the issue. Having a plan that you intend to follow, but you are willing to revisit and adjust, is not a bad thing.)*

That is, while there is value in the items on the right, we value the items on the left more.

Common Gaps, Environment Needs, and Tiny Details

Project setup. A common gap on many software development projects is to have the parameters of the project negotiated and to only then assemble a team with the mandate to complete the project as defined. This creates issues on multiple levels.

If the delivery team and the project manager (or the sole scrum master) are not involved in the project setup, then they have missed out on the opportunity to affect and manage one of the most important stages of the project—its initiation. Once the project is set up, the chances for success are irreversibly affected. Having participation from as many of the team members as possible is an important step toward minimizing risk.

Many projects are defined within a Statement of Work (SOW) that never gets presented to the delivery team. The team is simply handed a set of requirements and a final date. This is not the best way to approach a team if we want them to get to a high performing state. People can sense that they are not being treated equally, and predictably retract their full and committed participation in the endeavor. After all, if people are to develop a sense of ownership, then they need to be treated as proper owners of the problem. Also, important consideration in the form of assumptions and dependencies might get completely overlooked by the people who "crafted" the SOW, thus exposing the project to additional risk.

One of the first steps toward a sensible working environment on any software development project is to have the full delivery team familiarized and ideally involved with the creation of the SOW. This lays the groundwork for a participative team and improves the risk profile of a project significantly. The delivery team should define the assumptions which must hold true throughout the execution of the project, as well as they need to identify any major dependencies and risks that need to be worked out in order to have a realistic chance for success.

Project start. When the delivery team jumps into implementation work right away, there is a huge risk introduced to the project immediately. The likelihood for a successful project diminishes greatly when the delivery team is not allowed the opportunity to familiarize themselves with the business problems, main users of the proposed system and their primary pain points, and the typical journeys these users take through the current processes. Sometimes in an effort to save money, a select group of individuals will go over some of these topics and will produce written documents, only to then have the documents stashed somewhere out of reach of the delivery teams. People can go through year-long projects and then accidentally stumble on useful descriptions of personas, success criteria, and intricate flow charts with useful insight.

This is not what we want to save money on. Shared knowledge and understanding is crucial for optimal flow and a solid solution. A preferable approach is to take a few full days and have the delivery team and clients go over the pertinent items together. There are various tools for facilitating this process, and it is best if completed by a professional facilitator. An investment like this will pay off on any project longer than 2–3 months.

Project manager vs. scrum master. The job title, of course, does not matter. However, the attitude does. And the roles are different. Many Project Managers (PMs) approach project management remotely and do not immerse themselves fully in either the details of the implementation work or in the relationships within the team. A Scrum Master (SM) on the other hand has to be intimately involved in everything that goes into the team, and also be willing to serve the people on the team and provide assistance, guidance, or anything else that is needed to keep the team delivering great work. On the other hand, many SMs would refuse to expand sizable amount of energy on long-term or outwardly focused activities like project planning. An SM is mainly concerned with the work of the team within the scope of an iteration or two.

My approach, and recommendation, is to always care about the team first—not the forecast or the project plan. This gives a more useful perspective for the whole forecasting exercise as it becomes primarily a tool for helping the team and the project move forward. When the PM aspect takes precedence over the SM aspect, then the person responsible for managing the project might get confused that the forecast or project plan actually drives what is happening. This is usually contraproductive and backfires, as people and reality refuse to conform to the imposed plan. So for me it has always worked best to have the forecast and the plan be driven by what is the real capability of the situation, but fully realizing the impact that the forecast and plan have on the situation.

SCARF

"SCARF: A Brain-Based Model for Collaborating with and Influencing Others" is a model that is based on neuroscience and provides a useful framework for any type of social interactions, including negotiations. SCARF is an acronym for "Status, Certainty, Autonomy, Relatedness, Fairness," and the model is based around people's reward and threat responses on these five aspects of an interaction:

- Status—relative importance to others (in the context of the interaction)

- Certainty—ability to predict the future

- Autonomy—the sense of having control over events

- Relatedness—the perception of safety with others

- Fairness—the perception of fair exchanges between people

Here is how an intelligent and reliable forecast facilitates the practical application of SCARF within the boundaries of the project.

Status. Within the context of a project, the status of a client is that of someone who has asked for help in accomplishing something that is of value to them. And our status (the delivery team's status) is that of someone who has been entrusted with seeing their project to a successful end. When we promote the use and application of precise forecasting, we establish ourselves on the controls of the project, and we are allowing the client to take their natural status of someone who is being provided a service. This normalizes the relationship, triggers the client's reward response, and allows for the right type of interactions to occur throughout the duration of the project. It is their project, but they have already entrusted us with it, and by not shying away from the responsibility to control the project, we cocreate the correct social structure.

Certainty. By providing a clear outlook and prognosis, based on provable tracking data, we are delivering the ultimate in clarity and certainty to the client and to the team. When we confidently indicate the likelihood of not achieving a goal well in advance of the expected time, we provide the client with the opportunity to work out solutions while there is still time. And when we confidently state that there is a high likelihood of achieving a goal, we allow the client to divert their precious energy to solving other important problems. In both cases, we are triggering the reward response in the client—either by allowing them ample space for working out the project problems or by allowing them the comfort of actually knowing that things are on track (a very different sensation than the one provided by claiming delivery progress, but combined with continual inability of providing an outlook for the final result).

Autonomy. By providing clear and viable options for steering the project, we provide the client with the autonomy of choosing which option suits their situation the best. The client can steer the project where they want, yet still within the safety of what we have determined is doable. In this way we maintain the "status" aspect of the relationship, and we are still responsible for the ultimate effect that the application of a control has on the project, but we allow the client to choose which control to apply.

Relatedness. By being transparent in presenting the factors affecting the project's progress, and by openly providing multiple options for dealing with difficult situations, we show the client that we are working for them and that we are one team. With a willingness to let go of negotiations that have become inadequate for one reason or another, and by allowing clients to freely renegotiate scope while maintaining a clear picture of the involved costs, we become immediately relatable. Simultaneously we continually maintain the client's perception of our positive ability to carry out our part of the relationship. This shows that not only do we care, but we actually can, and will, do whatever it takes to get the job done (because we are basing everything on the provable capability of the situation).

Fairness. By laying down all the options, and by demonstrating regard for every percentage of throughput that we can apply toward the project's success, we create an environment where every action is treated fairly within the envelope of the project. Everything has a clear cost and a clear benefit. Choices have clear expected outcomes, and there are no secrets or intentional gotchas. By creating a fair playing field, we allow the client to have a reward response in this aspect of the negotiation as well.

Negotiation. The dictionary definition of the word is "*discussion aimed at reaching an agreement.*" However, I enjoy thinking about this word with its usage in the expression "negotiating turns" when driving a car, for example. This way, the whole project and all the people on it become one unit with an immediate objective of negotiating an obstacle. Negotiations on a software project take on a completely new meaning when I think of the word this way—it's a joyride.

Variations of the Intelligent Forecasting Method

Using a story map directly. If the forecast needed by business people is in broad strokes, this approach can work well. It is a good alternative to no forecasting when the relationship with the client is strong and the team is performing well. In essence it is very similar to what is described in this book.

This approach does not provide high-fidelity guidance for applying proper project control, it does not indicate trouble soon enough, and it does not (directly) facilitate differentiating "added scope" from "original scope."

Special care needs to be taken when mixing stories with clear definitions and stories that are vague or large. Another point to keep in mind is be vigilant about new stories making it into the product backlog—sometimes these are net new change, and sometimes they are a clarification for something that was already estimated.

All stories as 1-point stories. This approach is worth considering if we already have many stories that are similarly sized. Getting the whole backlog into similarly sized small stories can be difficult and expensive, though.

Something else to be aware of with this approach is that some stories are still going to be riskier and more time-consuming than others. If we do the right thing, and take on the risky and difficult stories first, then we might have a slower start. Plotted on 1-dot-per-story data, this will indicate we are tracking too slow for the project. We then need to convince people not to worry, since we expect to be going quicker through the 1-dot stories planned for later.

In practice, this method is better suited for iteration level planning and maintaining consistent delivery pace across iterations. It can save time in place of the planning poker game, and it also nudges the team toward smaller stories, which can improve the flow.

Invert, Always Invert

Carl Gustav Jacob Jacobi (1804–1851) was a German mathematician. One of his maxims was *"Invert, always invert."* He believed that the solution of many complex problems can be facilitated by expressing the inverse form of the problem.

By studying the inverse of the complex problem, we are presented with interesting options, and a valid solution often emerges. Here is how this principle is exercised in a few of the ideas in this book:

- To gain the ability to control the project with precision, we agreed to rely on things over which we don't have control and cannot evaluate with precision. By inverting the focus from precision to imprecision, we allow for valuable statistical properties to emerge in support of our objective.

- In order to be able to change the parameters of the project, we commit to a specific outcome, seemingly putting ourselves in a situation that does not permit change of parameters. By inverting the typical order of events, and committing before we know the exact details, we allow details to emerge once we are in motion and we are not simply working out a predefined solution, but we are actively designing the problem itself. In true collaboration with clients, we examine what success means and we adjust the details of its very definition in a way that supports the project's practical ability within a defined envelope.

- By inverting our focus from personal dynamics and high performing teamwork, and instead invest energy into developing a tool which is sourced from a place that seems diametrically opposed to the human aspect of the project, namely, statistics and scheduling, we allow space for the human relationships to develop around the critical supports of trust and safety (which are facilitated by the tool). This then allows high performance team dynamics to emerge and carry out the project.

I'm so much in love with the "invert, always invert" intellectual invention that its impact on me has not diminished in the last 4–5 years, and I keep rediscovering its beauty almost daily. Why I love it is because it helps create contexts that are capable of generating emergent solutions—solutions that take care of themselves. The contexts might be gentle and sometimes fragile, they might need special care to maintain, but what emerges from them is beautiful and alive. The building blocks seem very simple, but the emergent structures and solutions can get infinitely complex and complete— just like life itself.

Sample Spreadsheets and Charts

In this appendix are examples of spreadsheets and charts that we have discussed throughout the book. It is difficult to come up with a spreadsheet that properly reflects any scenario; however I feel that the essence of tracking and forecasting can be explored well with simple spreadsheets like the one here. And even if you do not use spreadsheets to actually generate forecast diagrams, the knowledge you gain from studying the basics will provide confidence for the conversations and decisions that you will have throughout your projects.

I have also highlighted some of the "formulas" in these spreadsheets, as this might facilitate understanding the discussions from Chapters 4, 5, and 6. If you are interested in the files themselves, they can be downloaded via www.apress.com/9781484250242.

Forecasting Project Chart

Figure B-1 is an example forecasting project chart. Scope renegotiation and project extension were secured in the middle of March based on the actual and projected performance. This is less than one-third into the project and allows people across organizations adequate time to adjust other plans and commitments.

© Dimitre Dimitrov 2020
D. Dimitrov, *Software Project Estimation*,
https://doi.org/10.1007/978-1-4842-5025-9

In this table, these are the more noteworthy details:

"Scope" is only looked at in the context of the amount of effort that is required to deliver the required function. "Current Planned Scope" represents the latest estimates. "Actual Complete Scope" represents that scope from the currently planned scope, which has been delivered. So, for example, if a large module has 10 identifiable sets of functions and the whole module was estimated to be delivered for "7 weeks," then if we have worked for 11 weeks, but we have only demonstrably delivered 8 of the 10 functions, the "Actual Complete Scope" can be roughly accepted to be 80% x 7 = 6 weeks. "Actual Cost" is however the cost that we incurred for 11 weeks' worth of work.

"Project Events" is a category of expenditures in percentage of the time in the day/month. This, along with the "Actual Available Effort," gets factored into the "Effective Effort" field. "Actual Available Effort" is the "amount of effort" we have at our disposal. For example, if we planned to have 10 developers available working full time on the project, but we only have 8, then the Actual Available Effort is 8. The unit here can be something else. In this particular project, all estimation was done for 1 week worth of work for two developers and one tester. So 1 week in the spreadsheet is "3 person weeks" worth of effort.

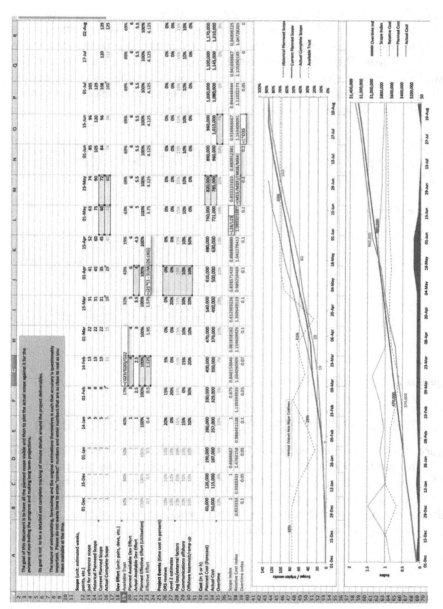

Figure B-1. The forecasting burn-up chart

T-shirt Reference Tables for Different Types of Estimates

Figure B-2 is a T-shirt reference table for different types of estimates. Estimating directly in days might not be the best thing when estimating a whole project but can provide a reality check during the project when more details are clear. The little reference table on the right-hand side specifies the T-shirt ranges in weeks of effort for three people. On projects where people work primarily in pair programming style, this type of estimation might be more adequate than single developer's weeks of effort.

Task	Detailed Estimate										
	size	optimistic	pessimistic								
Environment setup	L	1	2								
HTTP Redirects configuration	XL	1.5	3								
Capture the caller "prefilled" information on initializing for all 9 proc	M	0.5	1.5								
Populate the repository "personal info" object for the particular pro	M	0.5	1.5								
Submit captured data to API	M	0.5	1.5								
Pre-fill the payment related First Name/ Last Name	S	0.5	0.8								
Capture from data on each step for each product	XS * 3	0.9	1.5								
Replace Yes/No radio buttons with Agree checkbox	M	0.5	1.5								
Disable Next/Submit button based on checkbox value	S	0.5	0.8								
Change the privacy content around the checkbox	S	0.5	0.8								
Capture the number at initialization - for 3 products: GLP, EasyOne	S	0.5	0.8								
Add the AirMiles number to the API for final submit	S	0.5	0.8								
Populate the final call with the value of the AirMiles number	S	0.5	0.8								
CASL wording pop up window	S	0.5	0.8								
Sum-total		8.9	16.1								

Detailed estimates
XS range 0.3-0.5 days

High Level estimates
XS range 0.5-0.8 weeks (or even triplet-weeks)

Estimate values in days for 1 dev		
	optimistic	pessimistic
XS	0.3	0.5
S	0.5	0.8
M	0.5	1.5
L	1	2
XL	1.5	3

weeks effort for 2 dev & 1 qa		
size	best	worst
XS	0.5	1
S	0.8	1.5
M	1.5	2.5
L	2	3
XL	3	5

T-shirt estimation

Devs, QA and BA produce the T-shirt sizes only.

Sum-total optimistic and pessimistic to establish the estimation range.
Consider PERT calculation for realistic.

Adjust ranges as needed in order to come up with Calendar time.
Add other project activities to get an estimate for the whole project and not for the software implementation work only.

Use High Level estimation ranges when defining the initial scope of the project and do not have detailed requirements... error 25-50% (?)

Figure B-2. T-shirt reference table

Before Communicating Outside of the Team

Figure B-3 shows additional items to consider before providing a more final estimate number. Here only the numbers in the yellow cells are product of T-shirt estimation that was done by the development team. Those highlighted in red, along with the optional, need to be included when communicating outside of the team. (Make sure to be explicit about whether you are communicating **effort** or **calendar** time.)

	Optimistic	Pessimistic	Notes
more risk identification (optional)	1	1	
functional development	10	15	must have
QA manual regression	5	10	must have
QA ramp up	2	2	must have
external communication / delays	3	7	must have
internal communication / process (optional)	1	2	
ramp-up if new developers (no training) (optional)	4	6	
training if needed (optional)	6	6	3 days for the new developer, 3 days for someone to train them
status reports, demos (optional)	2	5	

Factor in additional team activities and add to the estimates provided by developers.

Sometimes QA and BA time may already be accounted for in the developer's estimation.

Total - must have	Optimistic	Pessimistic	PERT	Notes	Most Likely (PERT factor)	
java script developer	13	22	19			0.7
QA	7	12	10			
Dev 20% non-utilization (80% utilization)	3	5	4			

optional Totals	Optimistic	Pessimistic	PERT	Notes	
developer	8	11	10	ramp up/risk identification/training	
QA	-	-			
BA	4	7	6	Part time BA	

Contingency	Optimistic	Pessimistic	Notes
dev estimate error 20% (engineering coefficient)	2	3	may not spend but will need to have budget for this
holidays & vacations	2	10	not billable but a risk to schedule - need to have time for this

Risks (both prob and impact semi-random)	Probability	Impact (1 - 5)	product
CR not finalized	10%	2	0.2
not able to integrate within first week	40%	3	1.2
security - devs not able ot work in BMO network	50%	3	1.5

Figure B-3. Additional items to consider before providing a more final estimate number

Dev Sprint Burndown with Available Thrust and Technical Debt

Figure B-4 shows development work burndown with "Available Thrust" and with "Technical Debt." On some projects where people have high intolerance to lack of numbers, it might be cheaper to satisfy their addiction to numbers than to educate them and change their approach to work. By keeping track of accumulated technical debt, it becomes easier to justify lower velocity in subsequent sprints. Accumulated technical debt is quantified with the answer of the question "How much work would I have to do in order to refactor this and have a solid design?"

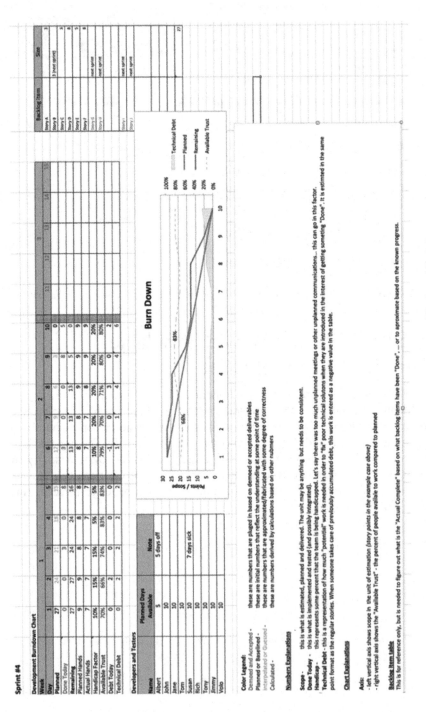

Figure B-4. *Development work burndown with "Available Thrust" and with "Technical Debt"*

B

Bibliography

Adzic, Gojko. *Specification by Example: How Successful Teams Deliver the Right Software.* Shelter Island, NY: Manning Publications, 2011.

Brooks, Jr., Frederick P. *The Mythical Man-Month, 2nd anniv. ed.* Boston: Addison-Wesley, 1995.

Cottmeyer, Mike. "The Case For Project Management." Leading Agile. October 15, 2011. www.leadingagile.com/2011/10/the-case-for-project-management.

Fried, Jason. "Why the Office Is the Worst Place to Work." CNN.com. December 5, 2010. www.cnn.com/2010/OPINION/12/05/fried.office.work/index.html.

Gilb, Tom and Kai Gilb. "When You Can Measure What You Are Speaking About, and Express It in Numbers, You Know Something About It." Gilb. November 21, 2016. www.gilb.com/blog/when-you-can-measure-what-you-are-speaking-about-and-express-it-in-numbers-you-know-something-about-it.

Hope, Jeremy and Robin Fraser. *Beyond Budgeting: How Managers Can Break Free from the Annual Performance Trap.* Boston: Harvard Business School Publishing Corporation, 2003.

Kelly, Allan. *Xanpan: Team Centric Agile Software Development.* Self-published, 2015.

McConnell, Steven C. *Software Estimation.* Redmond, WA: Microsoft Press, 2006.

O'Connell, M. Ryan. "Using the SCARF Model to Navigate Psychological Landmines of Negotiation." Viaconflict. April 30, 2015. https://viaconflict.wordpress.com/2015/04/30/using-the-scarf-model-to-navigate-the-psychological-landmines-of-negotiations/.

Shore, James. "Estimates or No Estimates?" The Art of Agile. August 31, 2016. www.jamesshore.com/In-the-News/Estimates-or-No-Estimates.html.

Weinberg, Gerald M. *Quality Software Management: Systems Thinking*. New York: Dorset House, 1991.

Wong, Joshua. "Change Management—The Subtle Difference Between Being Inert and Fickle." Integrative Thinking to Win. May 1, 2009. http://ithinktowin.blogspot.ca/2009/05/change-management-subtle-difference.html.

Index

I

© Dimitre Dimitrov 2020
D. Dimitrov, *Software Project Estimation,*
https://doi.org/10.1007/978-1-4842-5025-9

Printed in the United States
By Bookmasters